W9-BBY-958

TAKING THE HILL

PATRICK J. MURPHY
with ADAM FRANKEL

TAKING THE HILL

FROM PHILLY TO BAGHDAD TO THE UNITED STATES CONGRESS

Henry Holt and Company
New York

Henry Holt and Company, LLC
Publishers since 1866
175 Fifth Avenue
New York, New York 10010
www.henryholt.com

Henry Holt® and ® are registered trademarks of Henry Holt and Company, LLC.

Distributed in Canada by H. B. Fenn and Company Ltd.

Library of Congress Cataloging-in-Publication Data
Murphy, Patrick J., 1973–
Taking the hill : from Philly to Baghdad to the United States Congress / Patrick J. Murphy, with Adam Frankel.—1st ed.
p. cm.
Includes index.
ISBN-13: 978-0-8050-8695-9
ISBN-10: 0-8050-8695-1
1. Murphy, Patrick J., 1973– 2. Legislators—United States—Biography. 3. United States. Congress. House—Biography. I. Frankel, Adam P. II. Title.
E840.8.M823A3 2008
973.09'9—dc22 2007040643

Henry Holt books are available for special promotions and premiums.
For details contact: Director, Special Markets.

First Edition 2008

Designed by Meryl Sussman Levavi

Printed in the United States of America

1 3 5 7 9 10 8 6 4 2

To nineteen guys who deserved a government as honest and decent as they were:

SPC. SOLOMON BANGAYAN—Company B, 2nd Battalion, 325th Airborne Infantry Regiment, 82nd Airborne Division, Jay, Vermont, U.S.

SGT. AUBREY D. BELL—214th Military Police Company, Alabama Army National Guard, Tuskegee, Alabama, U.S.

PFC. DAMIAN BUSHART—A Troop, 1st Squadron, 1st Cavalry Regiment, 1st Armored Division, Waterford, Michigan, U.S.

PFC. JOSE CASANOVA—Headquarters Company, 1st Battalion, 325th Airborne Infantry Regiment, 82nd Airborne Division, El Monte, California, U.S.

PFC. MICHAEL DEUEL—Company B, 2nd Battalion, 325th Airborne Infantry Regiment, 82nd Airborne Division, Nemo, South Dakota, U.S.

PVT. MICHAEL DEUTSCH—C Troop, 1st Squadron, 1st Cavalry Regiment, 1st Armored Division, Dubuque, Iowa, U.S.

PVT. KYLE GILBERT—2nd Battalion, 325th Airborne Infantry Regiment, 2nd Brigade, 82nd Airborne Division, Brattleboro, Vermont, U.S.

PVT. JOSEPH GUERRERA—2nd Battalion, 325th Airborne Infantry Regiment, 2nd Brigade, 82nd Airborne Division, Dunn, North Carolina, U.S.

SSG. BRIAN HELLERMAN—2nd Battalion, 325th Airborne Infantry Regiment, 2nd Brigade, 82nd Airborne Division, Freeport, Minnesota, U.S.

SSG. JAMIE HUGGINS—2nd Battalion, 325th Airborne Infantry Regiment, 2nd Brigade, 82nd Airborne Division, Hume, Missouri, U.S.

SPC. CHAD KEITH—Company D, 2nd Brigade, 325th Airborne Infantry Regiment, 82nd Airborne Division, Batesville, Indiana, U.S.

SPC. JAMES LAMBERT III—Headquarters Detachment, 407th Combat Support Battalion, 82nd Airborne Division, New Orleans, Louisiana, U.S.

PFC. DUANE LONGSTRETH—Company B, 307th Engineer Battalion, 82nd Airborne Division, Tacoma, Washington, U.S.

SGT. FRANCISCO MARTINEZ—82nd Soldier Support Battalion, 82nd Airborne Division, Humacao, Puerto Rico, U.S.

PFC. GAVIN NEIGHBOR—3rd Battalion, 325th Airborne Infantry Regiment, 82nd Airborne Division, Somerset, Ohio, U.S.

SPC. ROBERT ROBERTS—A Troop, 1st Squadron, 1st Cavalry Regiment, 1st Armored Division, Winter Park, Florida, U.S.

SPC. MARC SEIDEN—Company B, 2nd Battalion, 325th Airborne Infantry Regiment, 82nd Airborne Division, Brigantine, New Jersey, U.S.

PFC. CHRISTOPHER SISSON—3rd Battalion, 325th Airborne Infantry Regiment, 2nd Brigade, 82nd Airborne Division, Oak Park, Illinois, U.S.

SPC. DOUGLAS WEISMANTLE—Headquarters Company, 1st Battalion, 325th Airborne Infantry Regiment, 82nd Airborne Division, Pittsburgh, Pennsylvania, U.S.

Contents

PART II
THE BRASS RING 65

PART III
TAKING THE HILL 179

TAKING THE HILL

PROLOGUE

What the Hell Is Going On Here?

JUNE 2003

It was after midnight on my first day in Baghdad when I was ordered to report to the office of Colonel Arnold Bray, commander of the 2nd Brigade Combat Team of the 82nd Airborne Division. For the next forty-five minutes, this tough 6'4" African-American warrior with two decades in the military—a man responsible for 3,500 paratroopers—described what I would face as the 2nd Brigade's judge advocate general (JAG) leading a Brigade Operational Law Team (BOLT). He was damn proud of what the six-member BOLT team was already achieving, but knew that there was a tough road ahead—and he had high expectations of our team, our mission, and me.

"Make no mistake, what you and your team will do—or not do—to win the hearts and minds of these Iraqis will save our paratroopers' lives," he told me. "Get out there, be aggressive, go after it." He described Captain Koby Langley, whom I was replacing, and praised his accomplishments in establishing a legal claims framework and cultivating relationships with Iraqis at the two courthouses in Al Rashid, Baghdad's largest and poorest district, where we were based. "You need to take this team even further."

As I listened, I couldn't help noticing the heavy bags under his eyes. Like most paratroopers, he was visibly sleep-deprived; three other paratroopers went into his office after me that night, each for an extensive meeting. I was still getting acclimated to the time zone and our spartan accommodations, and no matter how much caffeine I pumped into my bloodstream, I struggled to keep my eyes open that night. Our duty day would be eighteen hours every day. For officers, it was bad form to get more than five hours of sleep per night. Any less would lead to dementia, and substantially reduced reaction time.

My education continued at the 7:00 a.m. battle update brief the next morning. These briefings—updating us on combat operations in our sector the night before and what was going on in the neighboring sectors throughout Baghdad—were the glue that held our brigade senior staff together. Our intelligence officer told of a taxicab driver who had been taken into custody after trying unsuccessfully to fire a rocket-propelled grenade into an Iraqi police station. When questioned about it, the driver admitted that he had been paid to carry out his crime—two hundred Iraqi dinar, the Iraqi currency, still imprinted with the head of Saddam Hussein. The lives of Iraqi police officers—and the stability of Iraq—were being threatened for the equivalent of less than one U.S. dollar.

That afternoon, a man showed up at the front gate of our forward-operating base (FOB), located just off Highway 8, a six-lane concrete-and-dirt highway known in our sector of south central Baghdad as Ambush Alley. Shouting that we had killed his nephew, he demanded to see Colonel Bray. His voice was rising, agitating the crowd of over fifty Iraqis at the gate, who had already been standing in the hot sun for hours and were becoming unruly.

The guards called for an interpreter, and Captain Langley and I walked outside the gate, carrying our M4s and dressed in our battle-rattle: Kevlar helmet and Interceptor body armor (IBA) vests. We identified the man and walked him back into the compound, under the watchful eye of the gunner on our roof. As we pushed our way back through the throng, we could hear cries of desperation in broken English: "Where is water?"; "Why no lights?"; "I thought you great Americans?"

I was puzzled. Why was this crowd of Iraqis standing here baking in the summer sun? What were they asking *us* for? Wasn't there someplace we could send them? Weren't we just in charge of security and combat operations?

There were no good answers. All we knew was that humanitarian organizations were in full retreat due to the escalating violence, and Jay Garner, the leader of the so-called interim government, the Office of Reconstruction and Humanitarian Assistance, had just been fired. Thirteen weeks after our invasion and military commanders were left holding the bag, scrambling to create a mini Marshall Plan in the absence of support and direction from Washington and the Green Zone. The growing numbers of disgruntled Iraqis shaking the gates of every forward operating base in Iraq became a tactical nightmare. We were losing the battle for hearts and minds. An entire postwar reconstruction system had to be built from scratch—immediately.

I glanced up to the roof, eyeing the gunner, who was steadily scanning the crowd for signs of insurgent activity, and wondered, *What the hell is going on here?* These were trained combat paratroopers—the finest in the army. They had fought their way into the heart of Baghdad, and achieved one of the most stunning military victories in the history of warfare. And now they were being used to guard a base against civilians desperate for food, water, and some semblance of normalcy.

As we escorted the Iraqi into our compound, Captain Langley looked over at me. He must have recognized the look of incomprehension in my eyes. "Don't worry," he said, "you're a paratrooper. Remember: Impossible is our regular workday." I would later tell my team that we could spend our time in Iraq hiding from the reality, and the seeming impossibility of the situation, or we could spend it trying our Airborne best to make a difference. "They are going to give you some medal when you get back from this war," I'd tell them. "Just make sure you earn it."

When we got inside the compound, the Iraqi told us his story. Apparently, several nights earlier, the 82nd Airborne had conducted a cordon and search in an area where our intelligence indicated insurgents were living or operating. In that type of operation, U.S. forces cordon off a city block or two from pedestrians and vehicles, make a bullhorn announcement in Arabic that everyone should stay indoors, and proceed to search buildings in the restricted area for weapons, hostages, or suspected insurgents.

On the night in question, paratroopers planted themselves on rooftops, scoping out possible threats in the cordoned-off zone. Suddenly, one of them noticed an Iraqi male carrying a machine gun emerge onto a rooftop several houses away on the other side of the street. The Iraqi's head turned as he appeared to gaze down to where other paratroopers were entering the building below him. Even with night-vision goggles, it was hard to gauge from across the street what the Iraqi was doing with the weapon, but it appeared he was focusing his aim on our soldiers, preparing to fire.

The paratroopers got on their radios: "Potential target ten o'clock at southern rooftop!" "Potential engagement of friendlies." "Confirm weapon?" asked a paratrooper, not knowing how long he had before the Iraqi took his shot. The squad leader answered immediately from a nearby location, "Weapon confirmed." "Take out the hostile," someone shouted over the radio. Shots rang out from an M4. The Iraqi fell to the ground.

Within seconds, paratroopers rushed into the building and climbed the back staircase. Meanwhile, another Iraqi man appeared on the rooftop, retrieved the weapon our paratroopers had seen and vanished back into the building. When our troops raced inside a few moments later, the Airborne medic reported over the radio that the fallen Iraqi was a twelve-year-old boy, whose mother was now holding him in her arms, shouting in Arabic. The mother was hysterical, tears streaming down as she wailed, anguish on her face. She refused to let the medic treat her son, clutching his lifeless body to her chest and rocking back and forth. Finally she relented, and the nineteen-year-old medic checked the boy's vital signs. He was dead.

The boy's name, we learned, was Mohammed al-Kubaisi. The man who came to our base was his uncle. Colonel Bray is an old-school warrior, but at that meeting he spoke not as a soldier or paratrooper, but as a father. He took off his Kevlar helmet and sat with the boy's uncle on our ragged office couch. "I have a son of my own," he told him. "I know my words ring hollow, but please know that we all grieve for your loss." Colonel Bray placed his hand on his IBA vest right over his heart, patting it as he spoke to convey his sympathy. His words were translated for the uncle, and the pain on his face eased ever so slightly.

Colonel Bray knew his paratroopers were acting in self-defense in the dead of night, eight thousand miles from home. He was not going to second-guess them. Neither was I. When Mohammed's uncle first came to talk with us, he claimed that the killing was unnecessary because Mohammed had not been carrying a weapon. Later, he conceded that Mohammed had been carrying a weapon, but explained that the boy had only been trying to hide it—not fire it at U.S. troops. Perhaps this is true. But given the imperfect knowledge that the paratroopers had that night, our troops made the only decision they could have under our rules of engagement and international law; they have an inherent right of self-defense, and they perceived an imminent and hostile threat. In war, even the best judgment often has terrible consequences.

The whole case left me with a profound unease. It reminded me of the words spoken by Israeli prime minister Golda Meir: that when peace finally comes, it will be easier to forgive our enemies for killing our sons and daughters than it will be to forgive them for making us kill theirs. When Mohammed's uncle left our office, I felt—as I am sure my fellow soldiers felt—that we had just made our own mission in Iraq more difficult.

When Vivienne Walt, a *Boston Globe* reporter, caught up with the al-Kubaisi tribal leader (called a sheikh) a few months later, the sheikh told her that Mohammed's family had still not received payment from the U.S. government for their loss and was considering retaliation.

"If they don't pay our settlement, we'll kill four of them," he said, sitting in his office near the Tigris River. "The Americans are like a tribe for us."

Back then, most Iraqis would probably have disagreed with this sheikh and opposed attacks on American forces. Now, the majority of Iraqis believe it's acceptable to kill Americans.

•

I had come face-to-face with the deadly reality of the poorly planned Bush war. It was a cruel twist on the Pottery Barn rule General Colin Powell had invoked: The Bush administration broke it, but it was the soldiers on the ground who had to pay the price—picking up the pieces, the shambles, of the president's failed plan.

I forced this thought from my head. I was only a captain, and I was here to complete my mission and lead my team, no matter what. But I later learned that nearly every officer worth his or her salt in southern Baghdad felt the same way *the day* they set foot in Iraq. You did not need to be a brigade commander or a general to be aware of the hornet's nest we had stirred up. It was a horrible feeling, like being strapped beneath a slowly dropping pendulum ax, seeing death in front of you, steadily creeping closer, and unable to move to the left or right.

But we had signed an oath to support and defend the Constitution of the United States. We were there to fight, and we wouldn't back down, even in the face of impossible odds. It was that warrior spirit, epitomized in every paratrooper I served with, that George W. Bush and Donald Rumsfeld were no doubt relying on when they left the multibillion-dollar reconstruction plans on the cutting room floor—too expensive, they thought, and not sellable to the American public.

It has cost far more now.

•

When I returned from Iraq in January 2004, I knew we needed a change of course. In time, I realized the best way that I could help bring about that change was to run for Congress. Two years later, I became the first Iraq War veteran to serve in our nation's capital. The district I represent, the Eighth Congressional District of Pennsylvania, includes the neighborhood in Northeast Philly where I grew up, a kid who took fist fights more seriously than schoolwork. It was in that neighborhood that I learned the values—service, honor, family—that I carried with me as a law professor at West Point, as a captain in the 82nd Airborne, and today, as a U.S. congressman.

That is my story. And this is how it happened. This is how I took the hill.

PART I

THE NORTHEAST PHILADELPHIA STORY

What lies behind us and what lies before us are tiny compared to what lies within us.

—Ralph Waldo Emerson

The Northeast Philadelphia Story

My family history is one of the lost chapters in the larger American story. There are few family records. Even the tales that have been passed down by word of mouth trail off after a few generations. I do know that I'm an Irish Murphy on my father's side and an Italian Rapone on my mother's side. My dad used to say we came from County Cork. "That's where all the Murphys come from," he'd tell me. Maybe. But while I have a healthy respect for the lives my ancestors lived, when I look back, I don't see the forty shades of green where some ancient Murphy might have tilled the land, or the crumbling Roman ruins an ancient Rapone may have viewed from her window. I see something closer: the streets of Philly.

•

Every Sunday, from the time I was a little child all the way through high school, the whole family would make a pilgrimage after Mass to my grandmother's row house—a narrow, three-story brick house with a view of the city's skyline—on Aspen Street in a Philadelphia neighborhood called Fairmount. Catherine "Kay" Rapone presided, walking from table to table in the dining and living rooms to see if we wanted more sauce with our spaghetti. After years of marriage to my late grandfather, an Acme Markets manager named Anthony "Tony" Rapone, she always called spaghetti sauce "gravy," a common Italian-American tradition. But her own Irish Catholic identity was never eclipsed. Even the photograph of John F. Kennedy that hung near the staircase on her second-floor wall reflected her Irish pride more than her politics—though she never let me forget that President Kennedy was a Democrat. Strong-boned and fair-skinned, Grandmom would beam with pride whenever she mentioned that her sister was a Catholic nun, and passed her religious devotion on to my mother, Margaret Mary, or "Marge," who spent more than three years in the Immaculate Heart of Mary convent.

In her spare time, Grandmom would iron the altar linens for the local priests, sometimes taking a break when her son Joe Rapone stopped by for coffee with a few of his fellow Philly policemen. In time, Joe would rise to the rank of inspector under Commissioner Frank Rizzo. When Commissioner Rizzo became Mayor Rizzo in 1972, he gained a reputation for ruling with an iron fist—a reputation enhanced when he showed up at a riot with a nightstick tucked in his tuxedo cummerbund. Some feared Rizzo. Some loathed him. But after he made time to attend my grandfather Tony's wake, most in my family idolized him.

Before he entered the Philadelphia police force, Joe had been a paratrooper in the 11th Airborne Division. Joe's younger brother Billy, my mother's twin, had been a paratrooper in the storied All-Americans, the 82nd Airborne Division, as well as the 101st Airborne Division. After serving as an enlisted soldier in Vietnam, Uncle Billy worked at the Philadelphia Navy Yard until it closed down. Eventually, he took up fishing, became a golf pro in a Philly suburb, and moved in with Grandmom. Sometimes I think he's just trying to enjoy the life he felt lucky enough—and fought so hard—to hold on to. While we rarely speak about what he saw over there, his voice always swells with pride when he mentions the 82nd Airborne. As a child, the pride of an uncle I admired was enough to give the All-Americans an almost mythic status in my mind that I carry with me to this day.

On my father's side, the tradition of service is equally strong. My father, Jack Murphy, served for three years in the navy and has the tattoos to prove it, like his father, whom we called Pop-Pop, a Word War II veteran and Veterans of Foreign Wars post commander. Dad enlisted straight out of high school with his cousin Johnny Kelly, joining up through the navy's Buddy Program, a Vietnam-era recruitment drive that promised to station friends together. But after completing basic training and advanced radio school, the navy decided that these two buddies had been together long enough. So Johnny was sent to Kodiak, Alaska, and my dad was sent to Ethiopia. Unlike his brother Joe Murphy, who was in the army, Dad never got the orders to deploy to Vietnam.

Shortly after he was honorably discharged from the navy, Jack met Marge, a brunette with what my dad calls "striking blue eyes," who had been working as a bank secretary in Center

City. Picking her up at work for a date one evening, Dad saw two truckers whistling and honking at her. He ran to the truck, weaving through rush hour traffic, pulled the driver through the window, and punched him in the nose. I guess there's a reason Murphy is an old Irish word for "sea warrior."

A short time afterward, Mom and Dad were married. A daughter came along a few months later, named Catherine, or Cathy, after my grandmom; a year after that, my brother, J.J., short for John Joseph. Two and a half years later, on October 19, 1973, I was born.

•

I can't remember the first time I heard the legend of Patty Ward. His story is so familiar to me that I sometimes feel like I knew Patty myself. He grew up not far from my mother on Aspen Street, in St. Francis Xavier parish. His dad was a cop, like mine, a patrol officer, who'd ride him around town as a kid because his polio made it hard for him to walk until he was nine years old. Patty took his Catholic faith seriously, playing an active role in his church and serving as an altar boy in elementary and then high school. He wasn't the best athlete around, with his bad legs, or the best-looking, with his braces, but he was quick with a smile and had a heart of gold—and everyone knew it. During his senior year, his classmates voted him the nicest kid in school and he even made the football team. Everyone considered him a friend, but only one was lucky enough to call him her best friend, my mother.

When the time came to decide what he would do after graduation, Patty considered entering the seminary; such was his devotion to God. But his devotion to country was strong, too. In the end, he decided that with the war raging in Vietnam, he had a duty to serve. So he volunteered in the army and was assigned to the 92nd Assault Helicopter Company stationed in Lam Dong Province, in the central highlands of the Republic of Vietnam. He was a door gunner on a UH-C1 "Huey" helicopter, usually the trail helicopter that provided cover for the lead. Patty was tasked with making sure all the weapons worked properly. The lives of more than a dozen men depended on him.

His commanding officer, Chief Warrant Officer Bob Harrington, whose call sign was Bear, remembers him as someone who wasn't a good soldier, with his hat always askew, his uniform always dirty, his hands all greased up, and his shoes never shined. No, he wasn't a good soldier, Bear says; he was a great soldier. Always there for his fellow soldiers, Patty was a good kid who brought the compassion and smarts he'd learned on the streets of Fairmount to the jungles of Vietnam. When another soldier in their platoon got a Dear John letter from his wife confessing infidelity, Patty walked in to see Bear. "I don't think he's doing too well, we need to look after him," Patty said, saving that soldier from certain suicide, in Bear's view. On three separate occasions, Patty ran nearly one hundred meters across an open field under heavy enemy fire to rescue soldiers who had been shot down, carrying them on his back to his helicopter with rounds kicking up all around him.

But the thing that really struck Bear was what Patty Ward chose to do in his spare time. While some were getting into trouble, or playing cards, or not doing anything at all, Patty was always on Bear's case to take the gunship on a different kind of mission. Along with a friendly chaplain, Patty would spend hours trying to convince Bear to take their helicopter to "appropriate" food from their supply depot for the children in the villages near them—in one case, even being chased away from the depot by security guards. The children, in Patty's view, were the real victims of war. He'd go into the small villages along the rivers near their base or a nearby orphanage and hand out the snacks just to see their smiles. In his letters home or in the audiotapes he mailed, all he talked about were the children. My mother still remembers the requests he sent home—a box of cookies here and a bunch of books there—all for the children. Amid the horror and evil of that misguided war, he never forgot what the nuns and priests from the neighborhood had taught him.

More times than Bear can remember, they would be huddled around the radio, waiting on standby, listening as reports came in of American troops under fire. And more times than he can remember, Patty would pipe up, "Bear, it looks like they're having a tough time out there. Maybe we should go help them." It didn't matter if the weather was bad. It didn't matter if the mission was difficult. Patty was ready with an answer: "Most gunships can't get out there tonight, Bear, but they're not nearly as good as us. We have to go."

That's what he said the night of August 22, 1968. It was the time of the summer monsoon. Bear, Patty, and a few others were gathered around the radio, listening as a fierce battle broke out. A firebase was being overrun in Bao Lac, a post designed to provide artillery and firepower for infantry units operating far from base camp.

"Bear, they really need our help. They're down to fighting in the wire," he said.

"They don't have much time left. They've got no chance without us. Come on, Bear, find us a way to get there, you can do it."

A team was scrambled. Minutes later, they were in the sky,

flying low because of the weather. Due to crew trainings and pilot rotations, the teams got mixed up, and the wingman copter was flying in the lead. The North Vietnamese Army (NVA) were expecting them, and they flew into an ambush. They performed heroically, and when the smoke cleared, they had saved the U.S. firebase and annihilated an NVA battalion. But their wingman gunship had gone down. They'd lost four men: Captain Verlyn G. Meyer, Warrant Officer James K. McAleer III, Specialist David L. Ferry, and Specialist Patrick E. Ward, one of Philadelphia's own.

I try to imagine what it was like for Patty, perched in the door of his Huey behind that massive .50 caliber on that rainy night. I try to imagine what he was thinking when he saw his chopper taking fire—when he knew that this was how he was going to die. In those last moments, I imagine him saying a prayer—a prayer perhaps for his family and friends, but also for the children he'd no longer be there to care for. And then I say a prayer of my own—a prayer that I might, in some small way, live up to the legacy of the hero I'm named after.

●

I grew up in a small but meticulously kept row house with steps and a stoop we shared with our neighbors, the Rahns. It was a three-bedroom, one-and-a-half-bath home, with the same interior and exterior as each of the ten row houses on Nanton Terrace, our little cul-de-sac in Northeast Philly. Each backyard was small and fenced in, stretching to at most eighteen by twenty-five feet. Because we were close to the Rahns, who had three boys our age, we knocked down the fence dividing our backyards and installed an aboveground, four-foot-deep pool—one of the few luxuries we had growing up.

For most of my childhood, Mom worked as a legal secretary for S. Gerald "Jerry" Litvin, the named partner of his own prestigious Philadelphia firm. Like Mom's brother Joe, my dad was a Philadelphia cop. It is not easy being married to a cop—it takes a lot of strength and a lot of love. God gave my mother an abundance of both, but it took a toll even on her. "Always kiss your father good-bye," our mother told us most mornings. "You never know if this will be the last time you see him." Once, as a child, I stumbled out of bed in the middle of the night to find her sitting at the kitchen table, her ear pressed to a police scanner, listening anxiously for any sign her husband was in trouble.

Depending on the shift Dad worked—midnight to 8:00 a.m., 8:00 a.m. to 4:00 p.m., or 4:00 p.m. to midnight—my sister, brother, and I would come home from St. Anselm's Elementary School either to an empty house, a house where Dad was sleeping, or where he was ready with a hearty "How was school today?" When Dad worked the 4:00 p.m. to midnight shift, Mom would call at about 5:00 p.m. with the warning to "man your battle stations"—her way of saying the house had better not be a mess when she got home. After one of these calls, I remember my brother frantically gluing together a lamp that I had thrown at him during one of our after-school fights. My sister hadn't been there to protect me, and I, as usual, ended up on the losing end.

When Dad was home, we always knew what we'd have for dinner: either the "army meal" or meat loaf—his two staples and our only choices. The army meal was sliced hot dogs and baked beans, with white bread and butter on the side. His meat loaf was the classic kind with instant cup of noodle onion soup mixed in and a side of sliced potatoes. When he couldn't be home for dinner, our meals were either cooked by Mom or compliments of Swanson TV dinners. Dinnertime was 6:00 p.m., and my siblings and I were always given the chores of setting the table and washing the dishes.

Unlike Sunday dinners at Grandmom's house, where the men would always rush off from the table to watch the Eagles game on TV, this was Mom's house, and here she laid down the rules: no TV, no phone calls, and no reading during the meal. Dinner was family time. I've read that the Kennedy clan's patriarch, Ambassador Joseph P. Kennedy, used to lead political discussions at the family dinner table. That sure wasn't my childhood. My parents were focused on other things—such as coaching Little League, helping out with church carnivals and activities, and working full-time. It wasn't until college that I learned my mom was a Republican and my dad a Democrat. Politics just didn't come up too much at dinner, or any other time. After dinner, I'd rush out to play basketball with my best buddy Chris Norbeck under the glow of a streetlight that went on around 6:00 p.m. and had a basketball net attached to it—hoping the whole time Mom wouldn't find out I still had homework to do.

Like most kids, I formed opinions and picked up habits from my parents. When Dad was home, he would tell us to do our homework in the kitchen as he sat in the living room watching TV about ten feet away, separated by a dining room just big enough to hold a table and china cabinet. I'd listen to the news or the show he was watching—always more exciting than the multiplication table or molecular structure I was supposed to be studying. And I'd do as little homework as I could without prompting a call home from one of the strict Catholic nuns at St. Anselm's.

•

As a small kid and always rail thin growing up, I had a complex about not letting anyone bigger pick on me—a complex that often got me into trouble. One night, just as our family sat down to dinner, the doorbell rang. My brother got up and went to see who it was. "There's someone out here who wants to fight you," J.J. reported back. I felt the hard stare of my father. It wasn't disappointment; he just wanted to know the facts. So I dutifully explained that on the school bus that morning, a classmate had taunted me, saying a neighborhood bully could beat me up. I responded that he had it backward—I could beat that bully up, no problem.

But now the bully was standing outside our row house ready to settle the matter once and for all. When I'd finished explaining, Dad lowered his head, thought for a minute, and said, "Well, if there's a kid out there who wants to fight you, go on and fight him." Pausing for a second, he added, "J.J., why don't you go out there, too, in case your brother needs you." I flushed with resentment at the thought that I might need help, but was afraid and acceded to Dad's wisdom. J.J. followed along.

When I stepped outside, I could see a small crowd forming, neighborhood kids who I figured had heard there was going to be a bloodbath and weren't going to miss it. The guy I was about to square off with was feared by just about every fifth grader in Northeast Philly—and even some sixth graders. Within moments, we were standing on the curb, throwing punches with all the might our ten-year-old muscles could muster.

I tried to block out the sounds of the kids cheering from the curb and the taillights of passing cars. But then, a voice pierced through. A familiar one.

"There you go, Pat! Hit him! That's right!"

It was my father.

The fights continued as I got older. I'd play sports with the neighborhood guys, like me the sons of Philadelphia's bravest or finest, and often, in the heat of the game, tempers would flare. Most times, everyone would be fine, but there were rare moments when I'd feel the need to defend myself, which meant taking my father's advice and getting the first and last punch in—like I did when a teammate cut ahead of me for a drill during high school hockey practice and refused to apologize or give me my rightful place in line. But I also knew when not to fight. One late night, while dropping off a buddy at home, some friends and I were approached by two guys, one of whom had a gun poking out of his waistband. We kept our mouths shut and walked away with only our egos bruised and our wallets a little lighter.

From picking fights, I went to trying to prevent them. When I turned sixteen, even though I was just 125 pounds soaking wet, I persuaded the security guards at Veterans Stadium, home of our beloved Phillies, Eagles, and a few nearby university teams, to let me join their ranks. They gave me the unpopular and—considering my scrawny stature—inexplicable assignment of manning the infamous 700-level during Eagles football games, the section with the cheapest seats, most passionate fans, and most beer-fueled brawls.

One Saturday, a few weeks into the job, during a Temple University football game, I was standing with another security guard by our post when I overheard an urgent call for backup from our supervisor crackling over the walkie-talkie. When we reached the scene, we saw our supervisor, not a small man, caught in a headlock by an even larger fan. Momentarily forgetting that I was smaller than either one by about a hundred pounds, I plowed into them with enough force to knock our supervisor free, giving the guards who were just getting there a chance to pile on the fan, restrain him, and haul him off. The next day, when I showed up to work the Sunday Eagles game, I went to my normal spot in the 700-level, only to be told that I was in the wrong place. From then on, I was informed, I would be working near the field on the 200-level. It was my first and arguably best promotion.

Between my fights and my lagging performance at school, where I failed algebra and had to attend summer school, my mother was concerned about where I was headed. During freshman year at Archbishop Ryan High School, she sent me to work as a messenger at Murphy & O'Connor, a law firm that had employed my brother, J.J., in a similar role (we were not related to the named partner, Ed Murphy). When I asked if I could work at the Franklin Mills Mall instead because it was near our home and paid $5.50 an hour instead of the $5.00 I got at the downtown law firm, her answer was a firm no. This was not about the money. "You need a professional environment in your life," she sternly informed me. Mom was right, of course. Working at the firm showed me a place where battles were fought with reason, not right hooks. The partners even wore suits each day; at home, my father wore a suit twice a year—on Easter and Christmas.

It was exhausting. In the mornings, I'd often help my brother on his paper route by pushing a shopping cart filled with the *Philadelphia Inquirer* down the street, tossing copies onto neighbors' steps. Then I'd go to school for a full day of classes. As soon as the last bell rang, I'd take the bus and elevated train for an hour to Murphy & O'Connor. Often, after an evening at the firm and the long trip home, I turned around and went right to hockey practice at a rink fifteen minutes away in Bristol. I also tried to keep up my weekend work answering phones and selling Mass cards at St. Anselm's rectory, and later waiting tables at Perkins Restaurant. Occasionally, it caught up with me: I'd doze off during the train ride to deliver mail to the law firm's New Jersey office, miss my stop, and have to get off to board the train back in the opposite direction.

But the firm's larger-than-life leaders made it worthwhile, especially Mike O'Connor and Mike Dunn. They came from large blue-collar Irish Catholic families like mine, and even had pictures of John and Robert Kennedy on their wall. When I had to attend summer school a second time for cutting too many classes, I nervously approached Mr. Dunn to say I would not be able to come into the office that summer until school had wrapped up in the afternoon.

"Summer school," he said, "what are you doing there?"

I tried a stock excuse.

"You can't bullshit a bullshitter," he replied. "You're going to summer school because you're screwing around. Get your act together."

His advice didn't take; I continued screwing around.

When senior year came, even though we had only two relatives with a college degree, I decided to follow my brother and Mr. O'Connor to King's College, a small Catholic college in Wilkes-Barre founded to serve the sons of the region's coal miners. I applied and was rejected. It was a shock—not because I thought my grades would earn me a spot, but because I thought they would take me to play hockey with my brother. I had seen just one college team play, King's, and had applied to just one college, King's.

When I was rejected, and saw my high school drinking buddies apply unsuccessfully to become apprentices in carpenters' and electrical unions, and then have to find full-time jobs stocking shelves at the Franklin Mills Mall, I knew it was honest work, but not for me. Meanwhile, the two other high school students I worked with at Murphy & O'Connor, Mike Kelley and Steve Snyder, both excelled academically at St. Joseph's Preparatory School in Philly, one of the city's best Catholic schools, and had the pick of their schools when they applied to college.

For maybe the first time in my life, I'd experienced real failure. I wanted to prove to myself that I could succeed academically if I chose to. So I applied to Bucks County Community College. Even though I had to pay double the tuition because I didn't live in Bucks County, Bucks had a great academic reputation and a beautiful, sprawling campus in Newtown.

Another reminder that I needed to change my ways came on September 11, 1991, a date that would touch me personally again a decade later. I was still adjusting to the rhythm of a full-time college workload, working four different jobs to pay tuition and bills, and rarely had time to hang out with my drinking buddies. On this September 11, I gave up an invitation to join them at the local bar, which we always got into with our fake IDs. Instead, I spent my time studying in the library at nearby Holy Family University in Northeast Philly, ten minutes from my house, trying to get a handle on my new college classes. When the library finally closed, I came home to Mom and Dad's house and fell asleep.

That night, my buddy Bryan Lavin, eighteen years old and full of life, was out with our friends. He had recently asked my permission to date my ex-girlfriend, and even though I was still crazy about her, I said yes because I felt Bryan's intentions were honorable and that he had the decency to ask me man-to-man. It was the code my buddies and I lived by, and the type of guy Bryan was, loyal to his friends.

Bryan left the bar with our other buddy after watching the Phillies get beaten by the Montreal Expos, and ended the night, like we had done so foolishly so many times before, car surfing—getting on top of a moving car and letting the air blow back our hair as our recklessness gave us goose bumps and a sense of invincibility. But that night in an empty parking lot outside the bar, Bryan fell off. He hit his head hard and suffered a brain aneurism. He died a short time later.

I spent the next few days with my friends. We were devastated. And we also knew it could have happened to any one of us. Bryan's death changed us. We didn't stop partying; we still made careless decisions from time to time. But that night, I think most of us grew up a little faster. I know I did. Before, I had been so happy-go-lucky that I was aimless. Now, I knew that if I continued down that road, there would be no options left. I had to get my life in order. That was my focus now.

A Call to Service

At Bucks County Community College, I began to get my life on track. My first semester at Bucks was the first time I had ever made the dean's list. After a successful year, I reapplied to King's as a transfer student. This time, I was accepted and even received a small scholarship. I thrived in King's small class setting, double-majoring in psychology and human resources management, and eventually serving as student body president, captain of the hockey team, and as an Army ROTC cadet.

My decision to join the army seems inevitable in retrospect, but it didn't at the time. For someone who came from a military family, I didn't know much about military life—like the difference between an officer and an enlisted soldier, or whether a captain outranked a lieutenant. I hadn't ruled out the military: I'd thought about it from time to time, but not seriously. In the end, what drew me to the army was not just the memory of Patty Ward and my own family's service, but a chance conversation.

By sophomore year, my roommate, Todd Schweitzer from Toms River, New Jersey, and I were just barely scraping by to pay for rent and books. To make ends meet, we started working as servers for private receptions in Wilkes-Barre and as ski instructors in nearby Scranton. We couldn't even afford a car between the two of us and had to borrow a friend's car just to get to work. So when my roommate mentioned that by joining ROTC I could earn $150 a month, my ears perked up.

One day, I went along with him to military science class and soon became one of three students in King's small ROTC program. Under the guidance of two King's graduates, Captain Michael Dick and Captain Bob Thomas, a Pennsylvania National Guard officer who volunteered his time, we learned the basics of military life, meeting for physical training (PT) sessions at 6:30 a.m. each Monday, Wednesday, and Friday and, one weekend a month, joining our fellow ROTC cadets at the University of Scranton for field exercises such as rappelling, land navigation, and M16 rifle marksmanship. Military life seemed like a great fit: increased discipline, the focus on achieving goals, the sense of honor that came with it. It also gave me a constructive way to channel my natural combativeness. But my army career almost ended before it began. A routine physical evaluation with an army doctor brought to light that I had a heart condition that could disqualify me. I was nervous for a few days, waiting to see whether the army doctor would grant me a waiver, but he did.

That summer after my sophomore year, I flew to Kentucky for a demanding six-week-long training at Fort Knox. We were up at 5:00 a.m. every morning, and when we weren't sweating in 100-degree Kentucky heat, running hills with names like Agony and Misery, we were in hand-to-hand combat exercises under the ever-watchful eyes of Drill Sergeant Jeter and Drill Sergeant Little, whose sole purpose was to break us down and build us back up.

It was the first time I'd met peers from so many different backgrounds and schools—Harvard, Virginia Military Institute, and Notre Dame, a school that was legendary in the Catholic neighborhood where I grew up. I wasn't the smartest or the strongest or the fastest. But I held my own. And the experience gave me a new sense of self-confidence, helping me discover a strength, endurance, and knack for leadership I never knew I had. When I returned to King's that fall, I made it official by signing a four-year active duty service contract with the U.S. Army. Todd and I both tried to attend advanced training schools such as airborne, air assault, or northern warfare, but our small college was rarely afforded any slots.

The following summer, I traveled to North Carolina for my required training at Fort Bragg, also known as Camp All-American, home of the 82nd Airborne. It was a dream just to be training in the same place as the 82nd, but the experience was short-lived. A few weeks in, my shoulder gave out from an earlier hockey injury. I tried to stick it out, popping Motrin pills every few hours, but when a fitness test required forty-two push-ups in two minutes, I couldn't hide the pain any longer.

The verdict was swift. I would be sent home midsummer. My commanding officer was not even slightly interested in hearing my protest. I went to a pay phone with tears streaming down my face. Too embarrassed to tell my parents, I called J.J., now an Air Force ROTC cadet, and told him what happened. Being home under those circumstances was miserable. But I wasn't going to waste my time. I landscaped during the day, waited tables at Olive Garden at night, and tried to rest my shoulder as best I could.

As soon as I returned to campus for the fall semester, I went to see my ROTC colonel in Scranton. "Sir, let me have one more shot. I won't fail that test again. I promise you." "Okay, Murphy, I will. Get that shoulder stronger and don't let me down." My cadet colleagues would all outrank me, but I was undaunted. I knew things happened for a reason.

•

The most challenging test came at neither Fort Knox nor Fort Bragg, but in Wilkes-Barre itself one Friday night in December during my senior year. The night began where Friday nights in college often begin: at a bar. I joined Todd and our other college buddies, jokingly called the Cabinmen, at the Woodlands, a local bar that offered a $5 All-You-Can-Drink special that we usually took full advantage of. Piling into a college-sponsored taxi—one of King's anti-drunk-driving measures—we drove home to our off-campus apartment for a quick stop before heading out again.

Then the phone rang. It was J.J., who was on campus studying for his master's degree at nearby Marywood University. "Turn on the TV," he shouted. Every channel was tuned to an emergency broadcast. There was massive flooding, and fear the dike would break in the Susquehanna River, engulfing the city. All "able-bodied men" were called on to help fill and pile sandbags. All other Wilkes-Barre residents should evacuate.

Sobered by the crisis, I tried to rally my friends. "We've got to do something," I said. "Let's go down to the river. They'll need as much help as they can get." It was going to be a hard sell. Many of them were still drunk, and more interested in continuing the night's festivities. Their response disappointed—but did not discourage—me.

I called around to as many other friends and acquaintances

as I could find, putting my campus credentials to use. In my capacity as student body president, I called the vice president and asked her to rally each class president and ask for their help. As captain of the hockey team, I called my assistant captains and asked them to rally the players. As a member of Army ROTC, I called my fellow cadets and ordered them to help. I told everyone to spread the word that we would all meet in a central location: the men's dorm.

Thirty minutes later, I showed up with a few friends carrying all of the college's twenty-four shovels, which I had been permitted to borrow after assuring the maintenance staff that I would take full responsibility for each and every one. Gathered in the men's dorm were about ninety people, nearly a third of the three hundred or so college students who would lend a hand that night. It was inspiring to see so many people come together to help the community.

Chanting military cadence with my fellow cadets, we ran in the cold air from the men's dorm to the point along the river where we had heard that help was needed most. By the time we got there, it was about 10:00 p.m. As we approached, we could see mountains of sand along the edge of the road being replenished by municipal trucks. Our shovels would come in handy. We merged with the local volunteers already there, including a number of AmeriCorps volunteers, and took our place in the makeshift assembly line—one person holding open a canvas bag, another shoveling sand into a bag, another passing each along a human chain down to the river, where they were placed strategically into the water to stop the water surging up the river's banks. When I noticed a photographer taking pictures, I told him his time would be better spent helping us fill sandbags.

Finally, around 2:00 a.m., things were winding down and I

took my first break, walking over to the nearby Sterling Hotel, which was a hub for volunteers. I got a cup of hot chocolate and promptly fell asleep in a lobby chair. When J.J. woke me up an hour later, he told me everyone was going home. As we walked back toward campus, he teased me that I had slept through the whole night while he and the other volunteers were toiling away.

That winter saw the worst flooding since Tropical Storm Agnes struck in 1972, leaving water stains that were still visible high on the walls of the King's College library. From upstate New York to rural Virginia, tens of thousands of people were evacuated. The floods submerged homes and businesses, filling them with mud and debris after the waters receded. Roads and bridges were out—and so was the power. Telephone lines were down. Sewage systems failed. The governor of Pennsylvania, Tom Ridge, even had to flee the governor's mansion with his family. And when it was all over, the grim toll revealed lives lost, families devastated, and hundreds of millions in economic damages for the state.

One afternoon weeks later in late January a friend ran up to me during lunch as I was biting into a Philly cheesesteak and told me that the president of King's College, Father James Lackenmier, wanted to see me urgently. I didn't know the president well and had never been summoned to his office before. My mind raced through the possibilities of what rule I had broken or whom I had offended to warrant this summons.

When I stepped into his wood-paneled office, I was greeted with a smile and a nice hello. His warm welcome caught me entirely off-guard.

"President Clinton will be visiting Wilkes-Barre with the director of FEMA, James Lee Witt, and they'd like to make a stop at King's," he explained, adding that the president would be announcing an initiative by the federal government to help in the aftermath of the flooding.

I still didn't understand what all this had to do with me.

"Given your role in leading the student effort to respond to the flooding here in Wilkes-Barre, how would you like to introduce President Clinton?"

•

It had never seemed even a remote possibility that I would meet the president of the United States, much less introduce him at an event. But on the morning of February 16, 1996, that's what happened. When I had finished my speech about the "valley with a heart," I turned around to walk back to my seat onstage, and saw President Clinton getting up from his chair to walk to the podium. As I sat down, I heard him describe the tragedy that had brought him to King's. And then he said:

"We need to find ways to multiply the spirit shown by Patrick Murphy, by the AmeriCorps volunteers, and by the students at King's College if we're going to meet our country's challenges."

Hearing him speak that day was a turning point in my life. It wasn't just that the president of the United States publicly recognized my efforts. That was great, and it didn't hurt my social life, either; but it was a defining moment in my life because it stamped in my heart a duty to serve—to stand up and tackle our country's challenges. President Clinton spoke about the need for citizens—young and old, in Wilkes-Barre and across the country—to step up in times of crisis and lend their neighbors a hand. As I looked out at family and friends in the audience and watched their reactions to his speech, I saw in their eyes the comfort they felt from knowing their president cared about them. President Clinton was showing us what government can be at its best: something that offers help to Americans in need, and hope to Americans in despair.

For the first time in my life, I stopped thinking of government as some impersonal force that was run by faceless bureaucrats who made decisions with no bearing on our everyday lives. That day, I came to see government as the product of human hands and human hopes—and human errors. But I didn't have much time to think about that. That spring, I had more immediate matters on my mind—like earning my commission as a U.S. Army officer.

On graduation day that May, while my friends were driving home with their families or continuing their celebrations into the night, I had other plans. I was driving to Fort Indiantown Gap, Pennsylvania, in my $500 pickup truck for additional training and my second shot at the tests demanded by Fort Bragg. This time, I passed.

"Ten Years Out"

It's remarkable how a single question can change your life.

For me, that question came from Mike Dunn, my old boss from Murphy & O'Connor. We'd been talking about my part-time job at the Lackawanna Station Hotel in Scranton and my recent decision to contract with the army for four years of active duty, and I boastfully told him that after I earned my commission, I'd start earning $27,000 a year as a second lieutenant in the U.S. Army.

"That's fine," he said, "but what are you going to do after the army, ten years out? Are you going to come home and run a hotel?"

I didn't have an answer. I'd considered entering law enforcement like my father, but the fact was, I hadn't given it a whole lot of thought.

"Why don't you go to law school?"

I was taken aback, and actually a little embarrassed.

"Me, go to law school? I don't think I'm smart enough to be a lawyer, Mr. Dunn."

"Do you think I was this smart when I was your age?" he replied. I remember being astonished he had so much confidence in me. But after Mr. Dunn planted the idea in my head, it took hold.

•

I had already promised the army four years of active duty service after college, so I applied for the educational delay program, deferring my active duty service until after law school, and expressing my intent to enter the Judge Advocate General's Corps, the branch of the armed forces specializing in military law. Around the same time, I was accepted into Widener University School of Law, in Harrisburg, Pennsylvania. My first year at Widener wasn't easy. Since I was in effect taking a leave from the army to attend law school, I was no longer receiving the army's $150 monthly stipend. So I worked part-time selling bar exam preparation materials, and sometimes went with my father, who was working three jobs at the time (and still does to this day), to give blood plasma for $25 a week—something I was too embarrassed to admit to my classmates.

The courses were valuable but dry, and I decided early on that my education would not be confined to the classroom. The summer after my first year, I took a work-study internship with the Philadelphia district attorney, Lynne Abraham. At the time, the Philadelphia area was immersed in what was being called the Carnival Killing, in which a sixteen-year-old girl was killed in Northeast Philly by a girl the same age for nothing more than a dirty look at a neighborhood carnival. I asked my boss if I could attend the trial even though I wasn't assigned to the Homicide Division, and he said it would be a good learning experience.

At the trial, I wanted to be a part of the case. So I got up during the first break, went over to the lead prosecutor, introduced myself, and offered to help. I'm not sure what he made of me, an intern making a presumptuous offer like that, but during the next break, he waved me over and asked me to go to the law library and do some research in anticipation of an argument he expected the defense to make that the victim had been part of a gang.

When I brought him the research, he looked it over, smiled, and told me to show up at his office the next morning if I was interested in playing a more permanent part in the case. The other interns couldn't believe it. They assumed I'd pulled strings to get the job. But I didn't have any strings to pull. I'd asked if they needed help, and they did.

The camaraderie I felt with the prosecutors and police officers made working in the DA's office a natural fit—as did the premium placed on hard work. I'd show up by 6:45 a.m. every day and usually stay after nine at night, or later if they needed me. I lived with my aunt and uncle in Fairmount, since my parents had moved to Palmyra, a small town two hours away that is next to Hershey, which is known as "The Sweetest Place on Earth" because of its chocolate-smelling breeze.

My uncle would remind me almost daily how dangerous it was to walk home at night in a suit, because someone could mistake me for having money. But I told my uncle not to worry, that I often carried an umbrella and I'd stick it somewhere nobody would ever want if I ran into problems. Besides, I knew when to defend myself and when to give up any money I might have had. I enjoyed walking home in the warm summer nights down the Ben Franklin Parkway, thinking through the cases I was working on, finally using my intellect to solve problems.

It was a tight-knit office, and I learned more about becoming a prosecutor and our justice system in those few months than I did in all my years in college and law school. Many of the police officers who testified in our cases had worked for my father when he was a sergeant, and always went the extra mile on my cases, showing up early, staying late, and bringing their notes and relevant witnesses from various crime scenes. They also invited me to drive with them on police ride-alongs when they were patrolling, and I'd take them up on it during the weekends.

The following fall, a classmate asked if I was interested in working for the state government as a legislative aide in the local office of Pennsylvania State Representative Tom Tangretti, a Democrat from Westmoreland County. It was a chance to learn about local policy and supplement my income, and, best of all, I could stay late at the state capitol building in my quiet office cubicle and study.

One of the letters that crossed my desk was from a constituent, Mrs. Murphy, whose son was killed when he fell asleep at the wheel and drove off the road during a ski trip in Colorado. She was trying to make sure some good came of her family's tragedy and was writing to ask whether Pennsylvania's highways had rumble strips, the ribbed segments alongside the road that make noise when tires pass over them. As I read and reread her letter, I remembered falling asleep at the wheel one night on my way home from the Jersey Shore with some friends when I was sixteen, and how it could just as easily have been me in that car or my mother writing that letter. It still moves me to remember the comfort in her voice when I told her that Pennsylvania had a strong rumble strips program, and that Representative Tangretti was a supporter. A policy wonk was born.

•

The next summer, before my final year of law school, I worked for the U.S. Army's 1st Armored Division in Baumholder, Germany. Traveling a few weekends throughout Europe was exciting, as was the trip with my childhood buddies to Dublin and Munich. When I returned to Widener that fall, I decided to get involved in the Civil Law Clinic, a group of law students who provided legal services to Harrisburg's poor. Meanwhile, I was also helping kick-start the fledgling Widener chapter of the St. Thomas More Society, a national organization of Catholic lawyers dedicated to public service. Twice a month, we volunteered at the St. Francis of Assisi Soup Kitchen in downtown Harrisburg, handing out sandwiches, soup, and doughnuts to folks who had come to rely on St. Francis for their only full meal of the day.

While volunteering at St. Francis, I learned that the soup kitchen hosted a medical outreach program with nurses from local Holy Spirit Hospital. On a following visit, I struck up a conversation with a nurse and after telling her about my work at the law clinic, she suggested we offer our legal services at St. Francis. The next week, we set up a table at the soup kitchen and returned weekly in the months to come. We heard all sorts of problems—from sleezy landlords breathing down their necks, to government officials refusing to send their welfare checks, to mothers complaining about absent fathers. Sometimes we offered advice, sometimes referrals, and sometimes we just listened. Serving others felt like something I was destined to do. We didn't earn any money working at the clinic, but helping our clients improve their lives was reward enough.

When I graduated from Widener in May 1999, and passed the dreaded bar exam that summer, I was at last eligible for the JAG Corps. Mike O'Connor offered me a $20,000 signing bonus if I would opt out of active duty and go part-time into the reserves. It was a generous offer, but I felt a calling and I had made a commitment. I entered the JAG Corps on active duty and soon left for Fort Lee, Virginia.

•

Judge advocates are responsible for bringing justice to every corner of the U.S. military. And over the next three months, I was introduced to the core legal principles that would guide my work in the years to come. One of the perks of being at JAG school was that it gave me a leg up when applying to airborne school. That was the first direct step toward lacing up jump boots and becoming a paratrooper in the 82nd Airborne. The prestigious JAG school sent roughly thirteen of the eighty-four students in each class to airborne school. There was a competition, and I was lucky enough to earn a spot.

Then I nearly lost it. During a pickup basketball game in Charlottesville against students from the University of Virginia, I broke my hand. It was excruciating and required a cast, but I knew that if I showed any sign of weakness, it might jeopardize my chances of attending airborne school. So I asked for a soft cast and didn't miss a single PT session, doing push-ups with my cast on. A week before graduation, the executive officer called me into her office to tell me that I wouldn't be going to airborne school. "I just won't risk any further injury," she sternly informed me. I tried to protest. She didn't want to hear it.

My mind shot back to the summer I was sent home from Fort Bragg. It wouldn't happen this time, I told myself. I went straight to her boss, a more compassionate officer, and made my case as forcefully as I knew how, using five dozen push-ups as my closing argument to prove I was fit. A few days later, I began the long drive overnight to airborne school at Fort Benning, Georgia, arriving fifteen minutes late after my car engine blew out on the way. Even if I hadn't gotten it going again, it wouldn't have mattered. I would have run the rest of the way.

The first week at airborne school was Ground Week, which was spent practicing parachute landing falls (PLFs) by jumping off four-foot ledges while keeping our feet and knees together so we didn't break an ankle or a leg. We also ran what seemed like every inch of Fort Benning, singing this old airborne cadence:

If my main don't open wide,
I got a reserve by my side.
If that one should fail me too,
Look out ground, I'm coming through.
If I die at the old drop zone,
Then box me up and ship me home.
Tell my Momma I did my best,
And bury me in the leaning rest.

The following week was Tower Week, which we spent jumping off 32-foot towers, culminating in an exercise where we jumped off a 250-foot one. The Tower of Doom, as it was frequently called, looked like a bad sketch of the Eiffel Tower. High winds had sometimes wreaked havoc on young paratroopers-to-be, mangling them as they flew into the wrought-iron beams that served as the skeleton of the structure. No matter how many hundreds of practice jumps soldiers did, some would always forget to keep their feet and knees together, snapping an ankle or leg on the landing. Thankfully, I always remembered.

Next came Jump Week. It required five jumps out of a plane to become a paratrooper, including one night jump. It reminds me of the joke that, for some soldiers, all jumps are night jumps because they close their eyes the whole time. I vividly remember my fourth jump in combat gear. A young private from Oklahoma was sitting across from me in a C-130 airplane packed with jumpers. Puking into a barf bag tucked inside his shirt, a ritual he observed on every one of our five jumps together, he asked, "Sir, aren't you ever afraid?" "No!" I replied, stone-faced. In reality, my heart was pounding in fear, as I wondered what might happen if my main chute didn't open or I couldn't reach my reserve in time.

When we graduated from airborne school, the airborne first sergeant told us, "Two-thirds of the earth is covered with water. The other one-third is a drop zone. Some of you will have five jumps the rest of your career. Others will spend your next twenty years on jump status. But one thing is certain, you are all airborne."

For months, I had prepared for my next stop: Dongducheon, a strategically important city north of Seoul in South Korea, where I was being sent to serve as a judge advocate at Camp Casey. I planned to spend a year in Korea before—hopefully—joining the 82nd Airborne. But three weeks before I was scheduled to leave, I was called before my commanding officer along with another JAG and informed that Camp Casey was out. We were asked to choose between a spot at Fort Sill, Oklahoma, and one at the United States Military Academy at West Point. We both requested West Point. Fortune smiled on me, and I became part of the Long Gray Line.

The Long Gray Line

As I drove up from Fort Benning, Georgia, to West Point, New York, just fifty miles north of New York City, climbing over the top of Bear Mountain and coming around the bend, I saw one of the most beautiful sights I'd ever seen. Below Bear Mountain, down on the plain, was the picturesque campus of West Point, with its gray granite buildings, manicured fields, and the inviting Hudson River several hundred feet below. Coming from a college and law school, each with only about fifteen acres in small-town settings, I looked out at the miles of rolling green hills and it took my breath away.

Founded in 1802 by Thomas Jefferson, West Point had a mission to develop leaders of character for a lifetime of service to our nation. Soon, I'd be walking the hallowed corridors of Thayer Hall and across the emerald green plain where the likes of George S. Patton, Dwight Eisenhower, and Douglas MacArthur once marched as cadets. West Point is America's Athens and Sparta wrapped into one, and I was proud to be part of it.

There are three ways to become an army officer: ROTC, Officer Candidate School, or West Point. Like Colin Powell, one of my heroes, I was also commissioned through ROTC. But also like Powell, I came to love West Point as if it were my own alma mater, in a place he called the "wellspring of our profession." Duty. Honor. Country. Those were the West Point values. Our duty as professors would be to educate, train, and inspire the Corps of Cadets so that each of the 950 graduates embodied the values. "Making the harder right than the easier wrong" and "Fighting and dying when called to in war by our fellow citizens" were constant reminders of our warrior ethos.

●

As a general practice attorney, known as a legal assistance attorney, I was one of twenty-six officers, noncommissioned officers, and civilians in the staff judge advocate's office. We bonded quickly, but from the start I felt a bit apart, always one of the youngest on the staff at age twenty-six.

Within days of my arrival, I met with the other new officers and senior noncommissioned officers at West Point for a presentation by a three-star general. I had never even seen a three-star or lieutenant general in person. He was the superintendent, Daniel W. Christman, known as the Supe. He was straightforward and commanding. "Our focus is on winning," he said. "The American people don't give us kudos for being the 'Most Improved Army'—they expect us to win."

Under a personable and effective supervisor, retired Vietnam War veteran Colonel Dan Shimek, our small office gave legal guidance to cadets and retirees as well as to the active duty soldiers—reservists and New York National Guardsmen—stationed or retired near the military base at West Point. On everything from divorce to debts to wills, we were a one-stop legal shop.

The job exposed me to the real-world legal issues that soldiers face each day. A few months in, my long hours paid off and I got a promotion—not just in rank but in responsibilities. I would be the new chief of the Federal Tort Claims Division, a job defending the government in lawsuits filed from our jurisdiction—an $84 million caseload—from slip and fall cases involving some of West Point's one million annual visitors to charges of medical malpractice at our West Point hospital.

Immediately, I became immersed in a high-profile lawsuit. The suit had been filed by a West Point cadet injured while attending the annual Army-Navy football game at Philadelphia's Veterans Stadium when the lower-level railing broke, sending fans, including this one, tumbling to the field—a moment captured by news crews covering the game and replayed again and again on national television. Some walked away just with bruises, but this cadet broke his neck—an injury that ended his military career. The cadet filed suit against many defendants, including the City of Philadelphia, the railing manufacturer, the Department of Defense, and Secretary of Defense Donald Rumsfeld.

One of the first things I learned as a JAG was the Feres Doctrine, which gives every branch of the military what's called "sovereign immunity." That means the federal government cannot be held liable for injuries troops incur while conducting their military duties. The doctrine was established because otherwise we could have soldiers wounded in battle suing our government for their injuries. But the Feres Doctrine doesn't just apply in battle. Cadets attending a West Point football game are also considered to be on military duty. So technically, the Department of Defense was not obligated to pay the cadet a cent. I negotiated an arrangement stipulating the cadet would withdraw his suit, provided the army paid what would have likely been financially crippling medical bills. It was the first—and last—time I defended Donald Rumsfeld.

Those months were packed with cases and assorted legal assignments. I was working long hours and enjoying it. But I started to wonder if my increasing workload was a punishment for doing an inadequate job. One day I asked our staff judge advocate, Colonel Garth Chandler, a Mormon leader in his private life, if he was happy with my work. "Patrick, when you have a good horse," he said matter-of-factly, "you keep on riding it." It eased my concerns.

Soon I was tasked to be a cocounsel for the prosecution on a few military criminal trials, known as courts-martial. It was the sort of substantive and challenging work that I'd hoped to do since I entered law school. In one case, I prosecuted two cadets who had broken into a retail store and stolen goods worth tens of thousands of dollars. In another, I prosecuted a twenty-one-year-old cadet possessing a large quantity of illegal drugs. I often empathized with the cadets I was prosecuting, but the law was the law, and it was my duty to enforce it.

One case that really touched a nerve involved a math professor at West Point who sexually assaulted a five-year-old girl. The victim was a friend of his daughter and was sleeping over at his home when the incident occurred. We didn't want to put the little girl on the stand at trial because she'd already endured so much. So we had videotaped her interview with a military police (MP) detective the night of the incident at the hospital. Watching her explain on videotape how the assault had happened, in the simple vocabulary of a child, turned my stomach. We locked him up for several years. I only wished it had been longer.

•

Before the end of my first year at West Point, I had taken on an additional job as the Special Assistant United States Attorney for the Southern District of New York. Whenever a crime was committed by civilians in the jurisdiction spanning the Hudson River Valley region, it became my responsibility to prosecute it in federal court. In addition to the academy, the jurisdiction also included the nearby Veterans Administration hospital. One of my cases involved a man charged with assaulting a nurse at the hospital by, among other things, spitting at her. When the trial began, the defendant, a man of Irish heritage, surprisingly decided to take the stand in his own defense. Under my cross-examination, he claimed that spitting at another person was an old Irish custom, and that the whole thing was just a cultural misunderstanding. When I told him I was Irish, too, and expressed surprise that I'd never heard anything about this particular custom, he rose aggressively from the witness stand, asking if I wanted to take this outside. It wasn't the best idea for a man being charged with assault to threaten a prosecuting attorney from the stand, and I asked the judge to note it for the record. When it was all over, and the man was found guilty, the MPs who were guarding the courtroom that day confessed that they had been placing bets on how long it would take me to knock him out if I'd been allowed to accept his challenge.

It made me proud to be part of the law enforcement profession in which my father had served. And I could envision a career as a prosecutor; but the army had other plans.

Murphy's Law

Outside West Point's Arvin Cadet Physical Development Center, which had been renamed from the Arvin Gym because Congress doesn't like spending money on college gymnasiums, is engraved an often repeated verse composed by General MacArthur: "Upon the fields of friendly strife are sown the seeds that, upon other fields, on other days, will bear the fruits of victory." Its message is clear: The Academy is charged with developing winners for our nation, and the staff and faculty are expected to set the example.

While every cadet participated in mandatory sports intramurals, staff and faculty sports also reflected the institution's competitiveness. Throughout my time there, I played basketball, volleyball, and even ice hockey for a local team called the Fighting Suds, after their sponsor, Sweet Pea Soap Company.

I was also recruited to play softball in the West Point staff and faculty league.

The first game, they had me playing left field. I was nervous, trying to make a favorable impression on the other officers, most a few years older and of higher rank. I caught the fly balls hit my way, and when I came to bat, I hit a double, sliding into second base. I was thrilled to get on base, my heart racing from excitement and the thrill of a close game. When the next batter hit a single into the outfield, I rounded third with every ounce of energy I had as the coach waved me home. I knew it was a shallow single and probably a close play at the plate, and as I raced home, the catcher, wearing his chest protector, shin pads, and mask, blocked the plate, reaching out for the ball. I hustled and was three steps away when I saw the ball thrown from right land in the catcher's mitt without even bouncing. I knew my only hope was to knock him over. So I plowed into him. He stumbled and fell back, but held on to the ball. I was out.

But what I didn't know was that there was a rule in this softball league that you cannot under any circumstances plow into a catcher. The ump came running up, waving his arms and raising his voice. I was embarrassed, gave the catcher a hand up, and offered one apology after another. When the umpire lifted his mask, I realized who it was, Colonel Patrick Finnegan, the head of the Department of Law. There are only thirteen academic departments at West Point, each headed by a colonel, and each well known, like Colonel Finnegan.

While my teammates quietly thanked me for my hustle and told me not to worry about it, I was concerned I had let one of the JAG Corps leaders down in what may have been considered a cheap play. The next day I sheepishly walked into Colonel Finnegan's office, located down the hall from where I worked, and apologized again. I think he was amused that I was still so embarrassed. He assured me it was no big deal.

•

"Do you mind if I come in?"

I looked up from my desk. And then I jumped to attention. Standing in my office doorway was Colonel Finnegan, the ump who had chastised me a year earlier.

He shut the door behind him and got right to the point.

"We have a sudden opening on the law faculty, and I'd like you to join us. It's my understanding you'll be the youngest professor at West Point."

I didn't know what to say; I was completely unprepared for the offer.

For the past year, on top of my regular job at West Point, I had been teaching college night courses as an adjunct professor at nearby Mount Saint Mary College. My students were mostly military police soldiers and other enlisted personnel and their loved ones working toward a college degree. I taught whatever subjects they wanted to study, from Mark Twain to *Marbury v. Madison*, from Socrates to Sigmund Freud, or what I knew of them.

But it was one thing to be an adjunct professor at Mount Saint Mary and quite another to be on the law faculty at West Point. Some of the military's brightest minds—like Generals H. Norman Schwarzkopf and Barry McCaffrey—had served on the faculty at West Point. Colonel Finnegan also promised me that if I committed to serving on the faculty for two years, he'd help me get into the 82nd Airborne—something he had the connections to do. But, still, I wasn't sure. I was enjoying working as a prosecutor, and I was not eager to resign, as I'd have to, to join the law faculty. So I asked for the weekend to think it over and called my old mentor Mike Dunn. "Teaching at West Point is like teaching at Harvard," he told me. "You'd be nuts not to take it." His counsel was decisive. I took the job, becoming the youngest professor at the Academy at age twenty-seven.

A few months later, Colonel Finnegan held an orientation session for new members of the law faculty, where he explained what was expected of us. As professors of law, he told us, the core course we taught seniors or "firsties" on constitutional and military law was the first and perhaps only law course West Point cadets would receive and the only major interaction they would have with JAG Corps officers until they became commanders years later (or had a legal problem in the meantime). So we had a special responsibility to help mold the future officer corps of the United States Army.

The constitutional law section of the course was broken into three subsections. The first was separation of powers, which dealt with the powers of the judicial, legislative, and executive branches, as well as administrative power, and federalism. The second was individual rights, which covered the First Amendment, equal protection, due process, and fundamental rights. When this was completed, we moved on to a section on criminal law and military justice, which covered substantive crimes, those serious enough to be prosecuted by the government, and criminal procedures, including the Fourth Amendment, providing a right against illegal search and seizure, and the Fifth Amendment, guaranteeing a right against self-incrimination, as well as other rights. Teaching the course gave me a passion for constitutional law that I hope rubbed off on my students, and that I still carry with me today.

The fundamental principle that tied the course together was

the rule of law. At its core, the rule of law embodies the idea that every person is equal before the law, and no one is above it. According to this principle, political and religious leaders get the same treatment as the beggar on the street—at least, that's the way it's supposed to work. The rule of law stands in direct contrast to the rule of force. Throughout much of the twentieth century, this contrast was symbolized on May 1 when the former Soviet Union celebrated May Day, rolling out tanks and nuclear warheads in Red Square, while the United States honored Law Day.

I had been writing a biweekly column called "Murphy's Law" for the official U.S. Military Academy newspaper, *Pointer View,* and on May 2, 2003, I devoted the entire column to Law Day, which I called

> . . . an opportunity to highlight reliance on the "rule of law" as a means to achieve individual liberty and social justice. . . . Law Day should be important to all Americans and knowing about the law and the military justice system is vital—especially for those future leaders who are 29 days away from leading our nation's sons and daughters upon graduation. . . .
>
> On Law Day in 1962 former Senator Bobby Kennedy said, "In a democratic society, law is the form which free men give to justice. The glory of justice and the majesty of law are created not just by the Constitution . . . but by the men and women who constitute our society. Justice, in short, is everybody's business."

Because justice is created by "the men and women who constitute our society," I taught my classes, our laws were always growing and changing, and our Constitution was a living and breathing document. I also taught the principle of equality and spoke with pride that the U.S. Army had often led society in many areas of social change, most notably, desegregating our ranks years before our nation did. In this context I explained my thoughts on what I considered to be the misguided Don't Ask, Don't Tell policy:

> A member of the armed forces shall be separated from the armed forces under regulations prescribed by the Secretary of Defense if one or more of the following findings is made and approved in accordance with procedures set forth in such regulations: (1) That the member has engaged in, attempted to engage in, or solicited another to engage in a homosexual act or acts. . . . (2) That the member has stated that he or she is a homosexual or bisexual, or words to that effect. . . . (3) That the member has married or attempted to marry a person known to be of the same biological sex.

When I was my cadets' age, I took army regulations as nonnegotiable. When General Powell said homosexuality was a choice, volitional and not hereditary, and that other soldiers' privacy issues prohibited permitting gays into the army, my young mind readily agreed. But when I had been challenged years earlier to defend the policy by a King's College administrator, and had cited Powell's familiar argument, it fell flat. I had no recourse when the administrator described the movement for gay rights as part of the larger civil rights movement in this country. That moment at King's College taught me to think for myself, and I was determined to pass that lesson on to my students. When I started teaching my segment on Don't Ask, Don't Tell, I'd always take a poll and find that only about one or two cadets opposed it. By the end of my lectures on equality, usually only one or two still supported the policy, and it always made me proud to see my students starting to think critically.

Twice a year, I also interviewed prospective JAG Corps officers at Columbia and Fordham and other New York–area law schools, and I saw what a hot button issue this was. Often, an anti–Don't Ask, Don't Tell protest would greet my arrival. Once, at Columbia, there were students picketing, carrying banners. Dressed in my formal Class A uniform, I walked right up to them, introduced myself, and let them know that I was personally sympathetic to their cause. Today, the policy has become not only unjust but dangerously counterproductive: Since 9/11, it has resulted in the dismissal of more than fifty Arab-language interpreters and 3,500 much-needed troops at the very time when they're needed most. Sexual misconduct should be punished. But these wrongful dismissals were about sexual orientation, breaching our constitutional principle of equality for all.

•

After a while, whenever my students joked about my age, I'd tell them I was not as young as Alan Dershowitz, the famous Harvard Law professor, when he was appointed to the faculty at the age of twenty-five. But then again, I jokingly added, I'd been slowed down. "Alan didn't have to spend his summers crawling through the mud at Fort Knox and Fort Bragg."

However, my age did sometimes make me feel like the odd man out at West Point, too young to socialize with professors who were married with kids and too senior in rank to socialize with cadets. One of the few close friends I made was Major Lisa Vigna. We had tried a couple cases together as prosecutors and now joined the faculty together. Lisa had a five-year-old daughter,

Olivia, with her husband, John, a West Point history professor, and was a Southern-twanged, all-American girl from Georgia, and a Democrat in what seemed like a Republican bastion. Lisa always took the time to see what I was doing, and sometimes I'd join her on daylong excursions over the weekend. Once, she took me along with some African-American cadets to the Apollo Theater and the Schomburg Center for Research in Black Culture in Harlem. It was a small group and a brief trip, but it was an invitation to explore a part of America that not too many blue-collar white kids from Philly get the chance to explore or feel very comfortable discussing.

It was also at Lisa's encouragement that I decided to run a marathon in Hartford, Connecticut. When the day of the race finally came around, Lisa had dropped out, but I decided to stay in and run the half-marathon instead. The night before the race, I stayed over with a friend in New Haven. The next morning, we were late leaving and got caught in traffic on the way into Hartford. Through the car window, I saw runners a few blocks ahead; the race had begun. Hopping out of the car, I asked my friend to take the wheel and meet me at the finish line.

Joining the other runners for a few miles, I had barely broken a sweat when I saw everyone suddenly slow down and come to a halt. I had mistakenly entered the 5K. Hoping to find the half-marathon, I began looking around but quickly decided just to run the 5K three times.

As I was running back on the last lap, with no one in front of me, a complete stranger suddenly appeared by my side, trying to hand me a large American flag. I had no idea what he was doing and tried to wave him off, but he stuck with me. Moments later, I saw an immense crowd forming near the finish line. Onlookers in the stands lining the route began to rise from their seats and clap. Camera bulbs began to flash. When I saw the marathon officials raising the finish-line tape, I finally realized what was happening: My 5K route was the tail end of the full marathon, and I was being mistakenly hailed as the winner.

Embarrassed, I shook my head and waved my arms, trying in vain to explain the misunderstanding. Moments later, I noticed the poor fellow from Kenya, whom the local papers had forecast as the presumptive victor, trailing me by a few hundred feet. There were a few scattered cheers for him, but no American flag and only a few flashing bulbs. I cleared out of the way and let the rightful champion claim his glory. But I joked with Lisa when I got back that I was the unofficial winner of the 2001 Greater Hartford Marathon.

Eventually Lisa and her family transferred to Fort Leavenworth, and, a little while later, I received word that she had been diagnosed with uterine cancer. Over the next three years, she fought with all the entrenched, stubborn mettle she could bring to bear. After I left West Point, I tried to stay in touch to see how she was doing. Her battle was heroic, and it was inspiring, but it ended in sadness. Lisa was one of the 7,400 women who die from this illness each year. When she was buried at West Point—an honor rare for someone who had not graduated from the Academy—many of us came back for her memorial service at the old cadet chapel. We watched little Olivia place a rose on her casket, and we all had tears in our eyes.

•

During my first year at West Point, I learned that the Academy was holding an eight-event challenge, culminating in an 18.7-mile Ruck March that had to be completed while carrying a

22.5-pound backpack—all for the honor of an obscure German military badge. It was the kind of self-punishing exercise that soldiers take pride in. When I let a few buddies know about it over a couple of beers, adding that they probably wouldn't be able to keep up with me, every one of them signed up.

On the morning of the march, I loaded my pack with all the required supplies but one—I decided not to pack the 2-quart canteen the instructions told us to bring. It seemed unnecessary. I already had two 1-quart canteens strapped to my belt, and there were water stations along the way. So I hoisted the 22-pound pack onto my shoulders, stepped out into the single-digit December weather, and set off for the frozen woods along the Hudson River.

When I completed the march several hours later, blood and sweat seeping through my socks, the MP helping organize the march asked us to empty out our packs. One by one, he went through the items, checking them off his master list. Then he got to the one item I had decided not to pack. "Where's your two-quart canteen?" he asked. I told him I didn't think I needed it and had left it home. "Well, you have extra items in here, so as long as it meets the required weight, you'll be okay." He said nothing more, so I assumed everything was fine.

Alone later that morning, I weighed my pack myself. I was 0.3 pounds short of the required 22.5 pounds. The difference was inconsequential, but character is how you act when no one is watching. I called the MP, whom I knew because he was one of my night students at Mount Saint Mary College. He asked conspiratorially if I was sure I remembered what the scale read. "Yes. I'm going to do the march again—by the book." "You sure?" he asked. I was. In the steep hills of Bear Mountain, my feet still aching from the week before, I did the march all over again. This time, I earned the badge. No wonder my wife, Jenni, jokes that she married the last Boy Scout.

•

In May 2001, I took a much-needed trip to Cancún with my Northeast Philadelphia buddies. I was especially excited about it because the last trip to Cancún was during spring break of my senior year in college, and I couldn't afford to go. Even though I had an army scholarship and worked part-time, I had little left after paying for my law school applications, rent, and everything else. But now I was making $36,000 a year, more than ever before.

The trip was the brainchild of my best friend, Chris Norbeck, now a Teamster. As it turned out, it would be fitting that he had organized the trip, because it dramatically changed his life. From the moment he met Freehold, New Jersey's, Michele Hoffmann by the hotel pool in Cançun, Chris was smitten. And she felt the same. When they returned home, they started dating seriously. She had the same effect on Chris that my wife, Jenni, has had on me: She made him a better person. You could tell Chris knew it, too. The tone of his voice changed when he spoke about her. His eyes lit up, and his lips curled into a smile. You could even tell when he was thinking about her because he'd get this silly grin on his face, and you just knew he wasn't paying attention to a single word you were saying. More than once, he told me he dreamed of marrying her.

That dream fell apart on the morning of Tuesday, September 11, 2001. Michele and her father, Frederick, were killed along with hundreds of other employees of Cantor Fitzgerald, a global financial services firm headquartered on the 101st–105th floors of One World Trade Center, roughly ten floors above the first plane's impact. My college classmate from King's also perished that day. Our country, and our world, would never be the same. Neither would Chris.

I was at West Point that morning, teaching my 8:00 a.m. class on military and constitutional law in Thayer Hall. There was a buzz right after the first attack that a plane had hit the North Tower. We didn't know what had happened exactly, but most of us knew it wasn't some Cessna gone astray. In the military, you develop a sixth sense. Even to this day, when I enter a room, I always sit in a place where I can see as many people's eyes and hands as possible. I avoid putting my back to a crowd. These kinds of habits are ingrained in soldiers and cannot be let go.

As soon as class ended, I made my way back to my office, as usual. There was a somber air in the hallways. People were walking about more quickly, their heads turned down, their brows furrowed. As I passed a cadet on the pay phone in the hall, I heard him leaving a message on an answering machine. The cadet, dressed sharply in his white-over-gray West Point uniform, was holding back tears.

"Dad?"

A second passed.

"Dad, if you're there, pick up."

A few more seconds.

"Dad? I heard the Pentagon got hit. Call me and let me know you're okay. I love you."

At that point, I hustled to the cafeteria, where there were televisions turned to CNN and FOX News. Standing there, along with the men and women who would soon be sent to Afghanistan and, later, to another war wrongly fought under the banner of 9/11, I saw the images that are now riven into our individual memories and collective consciousness. Soon, a fourth plane would plunge into the woods of Shanksville, Pennsylvania, after passengers heroically stopped the terrorists on board from striking the U.S. Capitol or White House.

Despite our best efforts to keep things "normal," West Point transformed that day. The post was put on the highest possible level of readiness, Force Protection Condition Delta. Soldiers were walking around carrying M16 rifles. I even pulled guard duty on weekends. Access to buildings was restricted, vehicles were stopped and searched. I must have dutifully looked under hundreds of car seats, hoods, and trunks. In the hallways, you could hear cadets talking about a loved one who was missing or where they might deploy after graduation.

Along with sadness and anger, I felt something else in those first moments after the towers fell: frustration. With all those years of training, I desperately wanted to do something more. When I heard that volunteers were needed in New York City, less than an hour away, I rushed into Colonel Finnegan's office and asked if I could join them. He said yes, but when the call for volunteers was countermanded because no more were needed, I was back where I started—frustrated, angry, and determined to help.

As the hours passed, I began to accept that I couldn't assist on the ground right away, and decided to be as productive as I could in West Point. Stopping by the office of a colleague, Major Margaret Stock, whose expertise was terrorism, I borrowed a book on al Qaeda, which I stayed up all night reading. It became clear in a way I had never understood before how difficult a challenge we faced. Our new enemy, I learned, operated in the shadows of governments, served as an umbrella organization for militants, and had a global reach.

The next day in class, I told my students that in light of what had happened, the scheduled lecture had been postponed. Instead, I was going to teach them about what I had learned from the book on al Qaeda. I talked to them about political Islam, sleeper cells, jihad, and the Taliban—little-known terms that would become household words in post-9/11 America. This was a national crisis, I said, and they all had a role to play. They were West Point cadets, the best and brightest in our country, and they could make a contribution during this national crisis. I told them about my experience sandbagging along the river in Wilkes-Barre during the flood, and encouraged them all to go up through their chain of command and try to help with crowd control and other essential tasks in New York or Washington, D.C. We began our education on terrorism that day; but it was not until 2003 that West Point established its Combating Terrorism Center.

Later that day, September 12, I paid another visit to Colonel Finnegan. This time I was going to inform him of a decision I'd reached the previous night. I skipped the pleasantries. "Sir," I began, "with our nation at war, I don't want to remain at West Point. I want to be transferred to the front lines. Whether it's with the Eighty-second or the One hundred and first, it doesn't matter to me. I'll go where I'm needed." I knew we had reached an understanding that I would stay on as a law professor for two years, but given what had happened, I felt the understanding had to give. "And, sir," I added, "I'm planning to call the Pentagon to make this request. I just wanted to inform you of my intentions first."

"Patrick," he replied, calmly but firmly, "I appreciate what you're saying. And to be honest, knowing the kind of soldier you are, I wouldn't expect anything different. But I'll tell you this. If you call the Pentagon, they're going to call me, and I'm going to tell them I need you here." My heart sank, but there was nothing more I could do; those were my orders.

The next day, I sat down to write my "Murphy's Law" column and devoted it to the first major foreign attack on the continental United States since the British invaded Washington, D.C., in 1814 and burned the White House.

I laid out the facts as we knew them in those first few days:

> All credible evidence leads to Osama bin Laden. Known as the "world's most wanted terrorist," he is the leader of a terrorist group called al Qaeda, which is based in Afghanistan. . . . It is an umbrella organization, coordinating with other militant organizations or cells around the world. . . . This cowardly group previously carried out well-coordinated, multiple bombings, similar to the ones this week. They bombed two American embassies in Kenya and Tanzania, killing over 200 and wounding thousands in 1998. . . . Ninety to ninety-five percent of Afghanistan is controlled by the radical Muslim authority known as the Taliban. The Taliban has continually given a safe haven to Osama bin Laden.

Besides urging my fellow cadets to give blood, and discussing the challenges of trying stateless terrorists under U.S. laws, I also rallied behind our new president and closed my column with a declaration of full confidence in him. "President Bush has promised that our fellow Americans have not died in vain," I wrote. "Our nation was attacked because it is a beacon of liberty. Our Constitution and our leadership will not let justice and freedom be compromised."

As an epigraph for the column, I chose President Kennedy's prescient words to the graduating class of West Point in 1962—words delivered at a time when there was another insurgency brewing in another distant land unfamiliar to most Americans. "When there is a visible enemy to fight in open combat, the answer is not so difficult," he said. "Many serve, all applaud, and the tide of patriotism runs high. But when there is a long, slow struggle, with no immediate visible foe, your choice will seem hard indeed."

It was a fitting quote to describe the battle against the terrorists who had just attacked us. But even as I wrote that column, in the highest levels of our government, attention was beginning to shift away from al Qaeda and toward another adversary.

PART II

THE BRASS RING

An Army is a team. It lives, sleeps, eats, and fights as a team. This individual heroic stuff is pure horse shit.

—General George S. Patton

Task Force Eagle

From the moment I left Colonel Finnegan's office on September 12, I made it my mission to join the fight in Afghanistan. An opportunity to do so emerged when a student in my night classes at Mount Saint Mary College offered to help get me a slot at the Army Ranger School, where he had been a high-ranking noncommissioned officer. The Rangers were at the tip of the spear, and I knew I needed to be in much better shape if I was going to make it through Ranger School. So I bulked up on a diet supplemented by creatine and protein shakes, and a training regimen unlike anything I had ever attempted.

I also prepared in other ways. Over the next few months, I spent less time going over material for my courses on constitutional law and more time going over matters of operational law in combat, doing my best to ensure I was ready for the day-to-day challenges I would face—such as how to treat enemy combatants, and whether a soldier could fire back if an attacker was hiding in a mosque.

I was still at West Point that spring when Colonel Finnegan asked me to lead a team of six firsties to a competition in the Law of Armed Conflict at the International Institute for Humanitarian Law in San Remo, a beautiful town on the Italian Riviera. It was the first competition of its kind. Firsties would be tested in their knowledge of the Geneva and Hague Conventions and other international treaties, competing against peers from some of the best military academies in the world, including Belgium's Royal Military Academy and Ireland's Military College.

At first, the other teams were apprehensive about us. Just six months after September 11, the United States had already triggered concerns around the world with our treatment of prisoners from Afghanistan. A few days into the weeklong competition, a cadet from Belgium grabbed my arm and said, "Captain Murphy, can I talk to you in private?" "Sure." She had a look on her face that I'll never forget. She said to me as we walked away from the other cadets, "Why doesn't America give Article 5 hearings to those detainees in Guantánamo Bay?"

Article 5 of the Geneva Convention ensures that "persons, having committed a belligerent act and having fallen into the hands of the enemy . . . shall enjoy the protection of the present Convention until such time as their status has been determined by a competent tribunal." But the Bush administration denied prisoners these brief hearings to determine whether or not they were unlawful or lawful combatants, arguing that prisoners picked up in Afghanistan were unlawful combatants and, therefore, not entitled to the protections of the Geneva Convention.

When the Belgian cadet grilled me, my reply was "I don't know—that's a decision for those at a higher paygrade." That answer disappointed her—and it disappointed me. The practice is wrong. In 2007, as a congressman on the Armed Services Committee, I had the chance to raise the issue with Patrick Philbin, a former deputy assistant attorney general in the Bush Justice Department.

> PHILBIN: Article 5 tribunals were not required because al Qaeda is not a signatory [to the Geneva Convention]. So those who were detained who were al Qaeda were not entitled to that. . . .
>
> ME: Well, actually, sir, it's . . . whether or not someone's a lawful combatant or an unlawful combatant. I would agree with you that al Qaeda is an unlawful combatant because they don't adhere to the same rules that our professional soldiers do. But I would argue that that's exactly the premise behind the Article 5 hearing, to determine that.
>
> PHILBIN: The Article 5 hearing is to determine [prisoner of war] status. And [prisoner of war] status can only be for those who are signatories [to the Geneva Convention].
>
> ME: Right. And the argument that you and I will probably have is that just because Secretary of Defense Rumsfeld or whoever it was in charge said they're all al Qaeda, they're all unlawful combatants, that is not for him to decide. . . . And that is exactly why we have the United States of America

> signing on to these international agreements, to lead the world, to show them that we believe in the rule of law.

Unfortunately, by the time I was asking these questions, it was years too late; they should have been asked before we started detaining Afghanis without giving them the simple hearings. Even now, not every detainee being held at Guantánamo Bay is a member of al Qaeda or the Taliban. I believe there are some people being held in U.S. custody for possibly illegitimate reasons; a few may even be innocent Afghanis delivered to U.S. forces by bounty hunters looking to receive the handsome reward American forces paid for Taliban prisoners. The Bush administration's disregard for international law taught our troops the wrong lessons, as I would later witness firsthand. When our nation's leaders give the impression that it is acceptable to disregard the Geneva Conventions, Americans should not be surprised to see crimes committed against detainees by soldiers on the ground.

•

A few weeks after we returned from San Remo, I learned I wouldn't be going to Ranger School. Someone in the JAG Corps family had passed away, and Colonel Finnegan had been tasked to send someone from his team on a deployment to Bosnia to serve as the replacement. He selected me. I was disappointed; I would have much rather been helping fight the terrorists in Afghanistan. But this was the job that needed to be done. So, in May 2002, I left for Eagle Base in Tuzla.

The recent history in the region was traumatic. Situated between Croatia and the Adriatic Sea to the west and Serbia to the east, Bosnia-Herzegovina in 1991 was the most diverse and volatile place in the Balkans. When ethnic tensions in the region came to a head, Bosnia became the battleground.

On April 16, 1993, the UN Security Council passed Resolution 819, designating Tuzla and five other Bosnian cities "safe zones," and acted to disarm the Muslim citizens who had vowed to defend their homes. Nearby Srebrenica was another UN "safe zone," as was the nation's capital, Sarajevo. Despite the designation, Sarajevo had continued to endure constant sniping and mortar attacks by Serbian forces embedded in the hills overlooking the city.

Located fewer than thirty miles from the Serbian border, Tuzla was the third-largest and most diverse of Bosnia's cities—an obvious target for Serbia's ground forces during their unrelenting ethnic-cleansing campaign. For over four years, the citizens of Tuzla had braced themselves for the worst. The worst came at 8:55 p.m. on May 25, 1995, when a single Serbian mortar round landed in the center of the city, killing seventy-one children and maiming more than one hundred others. Two months later, the dreaded Serbian general Ratko Mladic marched on nearby Srebrenica and executed an estimated eight thousand unarmed Muslim men and boys, some as young as eleven years old. The slaughter at Srebrenica was the largest mass murder in Europe since the Holocaust. Srebrenica's sick and starving refugees, many of whom had traveled more than fifty miles by foot, fled to Tuzla and began arriving at the front gates of Eagle Base.

By the time I arrived, Tuzla was mostly stable, although we still kept off the grass because of land mines. The job of Task Force Eagle, as we were called, was to promote peace and stability in the region by teaming up with local police to collect illicit armaments in an effort termed the Active Harvest program. As a command judge advocate, supporting a brigade from the 25th Infantry Division—known as Tropic Lightning because of their base in Hawaii—I was personally responsible for a jurisdiction that ranged from Sarajevo to Tazar in Hungary. In addition to responding to locals who filed claims against the United States government for property damages or personal injuries they alleged we had caused, I also had several defense contractors throughout Bosnia that came under my jurisdiction.

At the time, the use of military contractors was an emerging phenomenon, but already it was causing problems. Soldiers resented contractors being paid $150,000 a year tax-free to do jobs like sorting mail or guarding our compound—jobs our soldiers had done as privates for $15,000 a year. It wasn't unusual to hear the contractor Kellogg Brown & Root (KBR), a Halliburton subsidiary, referred to as Kellogg Brown & Loot because of the high prices they charged our nation's treasury. The waste and abuse of contractors on base were evident. We cracked down as best we could; sometimes we found they were wrongly receiving free meals and medical services from our personnel, but it was difficult to obtain their contracts to determine exactly what benefits they were entitled to.

It was all the more frustrating because some of these contractors, outfitted in orange jumpsuits with "Security" in bold letters across their backs, had never served in the military—or were so unprepared that they might as well have never served, a problem we tried to solve, with limited success, by expanding their training. I instructed them on the use of force, explaining the circumstances under which they could fire their M16A2 assault rifles to protect our base. But because contractors did not operate within the normal military chain of command, they fell outside our law, the Uniform Code of Military Justice. When one contractor was accused of viewing child pornography on his computer, the FBI lacked jurisdiction to prosecute him, and our only recourse was to send the contractor back home.

What I witnessed in Bosnia was a sign of things to come. In September 2007, military officials acknowledged that contracts in Iraq worth $6 billion were being reviewed by criminal investigators. That figure is on top of the $88 billion in contracts and programs being audited for financial irregularities. This is why the first bill I coauthored in Congress was the Iraq Accountability Act, which called for transparency and accountability in how Iraq war funds are spent, and also called for the creation of a commission to investigate allegations of waste, fraud, and abuse by contractors.

Further, with a number of contractors in Iraq that has grown to 180,000—more than the number of U.S. troops—the problems are worse than tax monies misspent, as serious as that offense is. There have been repeated allegations of killings or injuries of civilians by private defense contractors. In September 2007, contractors with the firm Blackwater USA were involved in a firefight that left seventeen Iraqi civilians dead, reopening wounds from an earlier episode in which a drunk Blackwater contractor killed an Iraqi bodyguard for an Iraqi vice president and was whisked out of the country within thirty-six hours. Blackwater's reckless disregard for Iraqi life was partly a function of Washington's failure to hold it accountable under the law. As a result, I've fought for legislation that would mandate rules of engagement for contractors who carry weapons, as well as subjecting them to criminal sanctions under the Military Extrajurisdictional Act.

•

My best friend in Bosnia was Captain James Dean Culp. A former enlisted paratrooper, Jimmy was 6'3" and weighed about 235 pounds. While his stature was intimidating, his boyish and jovial attitude put everyone at ease. He was the only defense attorney assigned to Bosnia, and we quickly became friends. Although I had seen the sadness on his face when he couldn't reach his wife or kids on the phone, no matter what personal challenges he faced, Captain Culp would gut it through, working tirelessly for the soldiers under his watch.

At our post, we had a field medical unit with doctors and nurses. That is where Captain Culp went when it turned out he needed minor groin surgery that summer. The day after the surgery, he called me up on the post phone and asked if I could meet him for lunch in the dining tent. He had decided to discharge himself, and hid two large ice bags in his shorts to reduce the swelling. With his shirt untucked in an attempt to hide the ice, Jimmy had walked to the dining tent all the way from the medical unit—about a half mile—in ninety-degree heat. By the time he got there, he was pale and drenched in sweat. I sat him down and left to call the medics.

Before I returned, he fell to the ground, unconscious. With the medics on their way, I rushed over to see Jimmy being comforted by two Bosnian women, food servers in the dining facility. Assuming he was a heat-stroke victim, they were rubbing ice cubes on his large legs, arms, and forehead, one placing his head in her lap and the other kneeling by his side. "You are a special, special man," they repeated. "You will be okay, special man," When he regained consciousness, he looked up, heard the two women, and smiled at me. Without skipping a beat, Jimmie Dean grinned, nodded in the direction of the ice packs covering his crotch, and said, "You see that, Murph, I'm a special, special man." I could not stop laughing as I helped carry him out on a stretcher. No matter how bad the situation, soldiers always find a way to laugh about it.

It was also in Bosnia—of all places—that I fell in love. Her name was Ashley, and she was a lieutenant, an engineer, and a West Point graduate. She was intelligent and witty, loved foreign films, and had a thick Texas drawl. While I enjoyed military life, she was less than enthusiastic. Comforting her made me feel needed during a largely uneventful deployment.

I left Tuzla in early September 2002. On September 27, in my first "Murphy's Law" column after my return home, I summed up my feelings about being back and what we had accomplished:

> As I was touching down at Newark two weeks ago, returning from my deployment to Bosnia-Herzegovina, I couldn't help but feel an overwhelming sense of joy being back in the United States. I thought about the differences we—American soldiers and civilians—are making there and in Afghanistan.
>
> As part of Stabilization Force 11, we teamed up with other NATO countries to maintain the peace in Bosnia.
>
> NATO's arrival in 1995 ended a four-year war that killed more than 200,000 people and left approximately 6 million people homeless. . . .
>
> American troops played a vital role in this NATO mission. We stepped up to the plate and hit a home run with some impressive numbers.
>
> The Active Harvest program teamed with local police and often went door-to-door to collect illegal weapons, grenades and other munitions. In six months, the effort

> equaled the disarmament of an entire division's weapons. Additionally, more than 2,400 families in the sector returned to their pre-war homes and the task force cleared mines out of an additional 300,000 square meters of land.

•

As I returned from my first deployment, the world began bracing for war in Iraq, though, the nation would learn later, the drumbeats had begun much earlier. Within days of entering the White House in January 2001, Vice President Dick Cheney encouraged a preemptive invasion of Iraq at President Bush's first National Security Council meeting.

Cheney was not alone in advancing this view.

Immediately after 9/11, marine three-star general Greg Newbold, the director of operations for the Joint Chiefs of Staff, one of the most important jobs in the Pentagon, briefed senior administration officials on the plan to go after al Qaeda and Osama bin Laden in Afghanistan. "Why are you going into Afghanistan? We ought to be going after Iraq," was the alleged response from Rumsfeld's protégé, Douglas Feith, undersecretary of defense for policy. General Newbold, a straight-talking marine and career infantry commander who had led forces into Somalia, called these remarks "extraordinarily inappropriate." But Feith's comments reflected the views of his mentor. As the fires were still burning at ground zero in New York City, the Pentagon, and in the fields of Shanksville, Pennsylvania, Rumsfeld was also pushing for attacks on Iraq.

None of this should have come as any surprise. In the late 1990s, Rumsfeld and Cheney were both founding members of the Project for the New American Century, a neoconservative group that advocated removing Saddam Hussein's regime from power. But it was not until President Bush went before the United Nations on September 12, 2002, that the administration began aggressively making its public case for war in Iraq—a date undoubtedly selected to promote the myth that Iraq was somehow connected to the tragedy of 9/11.

The strongest argument against invading Iraq came years earlier from none other than Dick Cheney, who had earlier served as President George H. W. Bush's secretary of defense, when he defended the decision not to invade Iraq during the Gulf War:

> If we'd gone to Baghdad we would have been all alone. . . . There would have been a U.S. occupation of Iraq. . . . Once you got to Iraq and . . . took down Saddam Hussein's government, then what are you going to put in its place? That's a very volatile part of the world, and if you take down the central government of Iraq, you could very easily end up seeing pieces of Iraq fly off. . . . Part of it . . . the Iranians would like to claim. . . . It's a quagmire if you go that far and try to take over Iraq. . . . [In addition,] the question for the president . . . was how many additional dead Americans is Saddam worth? Our judgment was, not very many.

It was prophetic.

•

Most West Point cadets were excited about the prospect of removing Saddam Hussein from power, eager to prove their warrior spirit and leadership skills in the crucible of war. But not all. That spring, several months after I became the academic counselor for the Department of Law, a firstie with deep reservations about the impending war sought me out. She understood her responsibilities, but doubted whether she could serve in a war she opposed. Talking with her, even looking at her, you could sense she was in pain. Her grades were slipping, and the faculty was starting to notice; some wondered whether she'd meet the requirements necessary to receive her commission.

Toward the end of the year, even as she had started turning things around, she told me that the Commandant of Cadets' chief disciplinarian was reviewing her case to decide whether she could still receive her commission. She wanted to know whether I'd be willing to speak to the disciplinarian on her behalf. I said yes. On the day of her hearing, I made my case. "Sir," I began, addressing my colleague, "she may not agree with the war we're about to fight. But unlike some other cadets, she's thought deeply about why she is serving and what she is getting into. I would trust her with my own life and would be honored to serve alongside her." Ultimately, West Point decided to let her stay.

This cadet was not the only person I was counseling about the war. Ashley and I had been dating since we met in Bosnia, and in January 2003 she learned she would deploy to Kuwait the following month when U.S. forces prepositioned themselves for the invasion. She was unhappy about deploying again. I helped as best I could and tried to be there for her, even though she was thousands of miles away in Germany and I was stationed in New York. I couldn't see her off to Kuwait, but her parents, both wonderful people, flew over from Texas. I wrote often, as frequently as four times a week, because I knew how powerful letters can be. It would be six months before I saw her again.

•

I was also attempting to overcome a nagging uncertainty of my own, a gut feeling I never spoke about and tried not to think about. Given our history of conflict with Iraq, the anti-American rhetoric being spewed by Iraqi officials, the banishment of UN weapons inspectors from Iraq, the president's fierce assertions about the dangers Iraq posed, and especially my own sense of duty, I wanted to take the Bush administration at its word.

But, privately, doubts persisted. Once, while watching *The Chris Matthews Show* in my apartment with the Sunday newspaper spread over my lap, I listened intently as Matthews challenged the administration's rationale for war. It was a rare and courageous dissent, and frankly, it made me uncomfortable. I couldn't help shifting in my seat as he talked about the lack of judgment our leadership had showed in Vietnam, and how our politicians were failing us again. I had never met Chris Matthews, but he was from my neighborhood in Northeast Philly, had been a top aide to Speaker of the House "Tip" O'Neill, and had run for Congress. I respected his judgment.

After the show ended, I took out General Colin Powell's book *My American Journey*. I had carried it with me since my days as a cadet and, scanning through my yellow highlights and markings, I reread a phrase that caught my eye: "War should be the politics of last resort . . . you do not squander courage and lives without clear purpose, without the country's backing, and without full commitment." That is part of what has become known as the Powell Doctrine, which requires that several questions be answered in the affirmative before military force is used:

Is there a clear threat to America's national security?
Have all nonviolent options been exhausted?
Is there a clear exit strategy?
Will overwhelming force be used to defeat the enemy?
Are the American people fully behind it?

I asked myself those questions, trying to answer them with facts I'd gleaned from reading everything I could get my hands on. But my doubts were put to rest by General Powell himself when I read what he had said that spring at the World Economic Forum in Switzerland:

> We have gone forth from our shores repeatedly over the last hundred years, and we've done this as recently as the last year in Afghanistan and put wonderful young men and women at risk, many of whom have lost their lives, and we have asked for nothing except enough ground to bury them in, and otherwise we have returned home to . . . live our own lives in peace. But there comes a time when soft power or talking with evil will not work, where, unfortunately, hard power is the only thing that works.

I trusted General Powell. If he thought the war was a good idea, then I did, too. If President Bush was taking his guidance, then I assumed the war would be fought wisely. What I did not know was General Powell was misled and his influence in the Bush administration was waning. He would leave the administration by the end of Bush's first term.

•

Around the same time, an envelope arrived, postmarked Afghanistan. I tore it open, assuming it was an army buddy or former West Point student.

"Welcome to the Division," the handwritten note began. "This will be the best job of your career. Be ready on day one."

That was how I learned I had been accepted into the 82nd Airborne.

The letter was signed by Colonel Tom Ayres, a hard-charging former West Point infantryman and staff judge advocate of the 82nd Airborne Division. His brief note said all I needed to know: The average PT score in the Division is perfect; and dropping out during a division-wide run is not an option.

It always seemed that there was no greater privilege than to be a paratrooper in the 82nd—a view formed in childhood chats with my uncle Billy. The All-American Unit received its nickname early on because its members came from every state in the union. The 82nd today is the country's 9-1-1 strike force, with fifteen thousand paratroopers dressed in maroon berets, high-and-tight shaved haircuts, and jump boots—and ready to jump out of a C-130 airplane and land anywhere in the world within seventy-two hours. Imagine being able to parachute one thousand American paratroopers and their equipment into a hostile drop zone and know within four hours that it was secure. That is what they trained for. "You can sleep well tonight," reads a billboard near Fort Bragg, "because the 82d Airborne Division, America's Strategic Strike Force, is on point."

Ever since I was an ROTC cadet, I had tried to build the credentials that would line me up for an assignment with the 82nd. During my first year at West Point, I had signed up to be one of four officers in air assault school—a school taught by the

All-Americans' sister unit, the 101st Airborne Division, at Fort Campbell, Kentucky. It was a tough ten days, and because I was the first judge advocate stationed at West Point in twenty years to attend the school, the 101st air assault sergeants delighted in picking me—the old guy—out from hundreds of the eighteen-to-twenty-two-year-old cadets for extra push-ups or flutter kicks. By the end, I'd learned advanced war-fighting tactics such as how to set up a helicopter landing zone at night or how to rappel from Blackhawk helicopters. It certainly hadn't been easy, but getting that letter from Colonel Ayres made it all worth it.

The day after West Point's commencement ceremony, my army buddy and fellow professor Tom Rooney helped me pack my rented U-Haul, and I drove through the night, arriving at 3:00 a.m. in Fayetteville, North Carolina, home of Fort Bragg. My brother, J.J., stationed hours away at Langley Air Force Base in Virginia, met me there to help me unpack.

As the new chief of operational law in the staff judge advocate's office, I assumed I would be stationed at Fort Bragg for at least a few months. So I leased a small one-bedroom nearby and began to settle in. My first day was typical. Starting out with a 6:15 a.m. formation for physical training (PT), we were expected to prove our physical prowess. Staff Sergeant Couch, a fireplug of a man, led PT immediately after that morning's reveille, the official start of the duty day, when the American flag is hoisted up the flagpole and the bugler plays his familiar melody while small platoon-size groups of thirty to forty paratroopers assemble, standing at attention and saluting the Stars and Stripes.

The first day of PT made clear why the staff judge advocate's office had the best PT score on post. The twelve attorneys and fifteen paralegal specialists were warriors. Sergeant Couch started

PT with four-count cadence push-ups. When he shouted "one," all of us went down, our chest and chins just inches above the ground. At "two," we all pushed ourselves back up. At "three," we went back down again, and on "four," we all came back up shouting "one" to signal that we had done our first complete count. There would be twenty-four more counts in our first set.

We did four sets of push-ups—wide-arm push-ups, diamond push-ups, and two sets of regular push-ups—each set followed by strenuous abdominal exercise. Then we ran. It was like running with deer. Years earlier, I was proud to run two miles in eleven minutes, fifty-six seconds. Here, that was slow. We ran five miles, many in a sandy part of Fort Bragg. Not knowing where I was running, I stayed in the middle of the pack. Toward the end of the five miles, as we headed back to where we'd started, I decided to finish strong. I pushed myself, passing a few paratroopers and finishing in the top half of our group, almost vomiting from the exertion.

Later that day, I attended an orientation for new senior noncommissioned officers and officers, called the Airborne Leaders Course. One of the briefers was the commanding general of the division, Major General Chuck Swannack, a square-jawed infantryman and West Point graduate, whom I had served under in Bosnia. The standard for a paratrooper, he told us, was to jump out of a plane once a quarter; but he added that real paratroopers jump once a month. That became my goal.

The pride I felt during that first week at Fort Bragg is undiminished today. The rear license plate on my car has an 82nd Airborne frame. Every day, I wear a small 82nd pin on my lapel. Hanging near my office door is a big American flag from Fort Bragg. And whenever my uncle Billy and I see each other, we still give each other the same old 82nd greeting.

"Yo, all the way!"
"Yo, Airborne!"

•

The several months I had planned to spend at Fort Bragg before deploying turned into several weeks. Just days after my arrival, I learned that the 2nd Brigade Combat Team of the 82nd Airborne Division in Baghdad needed a captain to serve as their JAG. It was a coveted job—one of only three brigade prosecutors in the entire division, and one that involved serving as part of the senior leadership team. The 2nd brigade Combat Team was one of thirty-three brigade combat teams (BCT) in the U.S. Army, each comprising between 3,500 and 4,000 soldiers—with sixteen BCTs in Iraq, two in Afghanistan, two in South Korea, and one in Bosnia. I knew most of the other captains in our office would be gunning for this position as well. So I tracked down Colonel Tom Ayres. Like other soldiers I would come to know, he was tough but fair, and I knew he'd at least listen to what I had to say.

Marching to his office, I knocked on his door and formally stood at "parade rest" with my hands folded behind my back, eyes straight ahead. When he invited me in, I asked to "speak freely" and made my case for why I should be selected, arguing that I had already served as a command judge advocate abroad in Bosnia. Two weeks later, I received my deployment orders. I was honored and, frankly, a little scared. Although I had trained and qualified "expert" on the M16A2 rifle, able to hit targets as far as three hundred meters away, I had never even fired the new M4 rifle, the Army Airborne's weapon of choice for close quarters combat with a much lighter and smaller stock; and I had time for only one visit to the rifle range before I left. It was not altogether successful. Firing expert on the M4 proved difficult, though I was relieved to hear that those who could shoot expert with the M16A2 rifle frequently had trouble at first with the M4.

All my remaining free time was eaten up taking care of last-minute business, tasks like finding friends to look after my car and apartment. I also had to draw up a Last Will and Testament, a rite of passage and a command requirement for every soldier deploying to Iraq. Meanwhile, I was trying to figure out what to pack for Iraq. Captain Koby Langley, the officer I would be replacing, sent me an e-mail offering his advice on the subject:

> You want to know what to bring? When we got to Iraq at the start of the War, I dug my own shit holes, wore my Bullet Proof Vest to my bed in the sand. I lived out of the ruck-sack I packed back at Bragg prior to the start of the War. I had two uniforms, slept with my M4 locked and loaded, and went through about two tons of wet-wipes. I got at least 4 hours of sleep in order to avoid dementia, and didn't bathe for 62 days. Our CP was attacked in As Samawah a month back, and we were just recently mortared, so I started sleeping with my Kevlar Helmet on. Things are a little different now—the engineers have dug a shit trench in the sand out back in our CP here in Baghdad, and laid a nice piece of plywood over it with four large openings. I don't have to dig my own shit holes anymore.

That was my introduction to Captain Langley. I was told that I should be honored he'd e-mailed me at all because he had a policy of not talking to new officers until they had served at least six months in the division. He later told me he had made an exception and talked to me because he didn't want me to get killed. I was glad to hear it.

But I got the message. So I packed only the essentials: two sets of uniforms, ten brown T-shirts, ten pairs of socks, one set of civilian clothes, a few photos of my family and Ashley, and two books, *The Uniform Code of Military Justice* and *Gates of Fire,* a novel about the ancient battle of Thermopylae. Not receiving any instructions one way or the other, and having already gone to the trouble of adjusting my rifle's calibrations, I also packed my M4.

Like most of my fellow soldiers, I knew little about what conditions were actually like in Iraq. There were no detailed briefings, no in-depth conversations with commanders or veterans. What I did know—or thought I knew—was that major combat operations were over. That's what the president had said several weeks earlier, on May 1, 2003, when he'd stood on the flight deck of the USS *Abraham Lincoln* in front of a banner declaring "Mission Accomplished," a banner he later claimed was the navy's idea. The lack of guidance was a bad omen. But I conducted what little self-preparation I could, searching on our classified computer server for the basics about Islam, Sunnis, and Shia.

I also had a farewell lunch with my family in Virginia, not far from where J.J. was stationed. J.J. and I had grown especially close and had been talking a few times a week about the war. As I said my good-byes after the meal, my mom, usually unflappable, started to tear up. I didn't want to get all mushy, and told her it would be okay. I hugged her and my dad, his face now flushed with emotion. I could feel the lump in my throat getting tighter and tighter. For my parents' sake, I tried to project confidence, but we all remembered Patty Ward.

•

It was late June when I left for Iraq. The night before, I went to a session of officer professional development. These were commonplace in the army, where the mid- to junior officers in an office get together for an hour-long block of instruction, usually from a senior member. Because my deployment was the next day, my attendance was not expected, but I decided to go anyway, because it was being led by Colonel Ayers, and I wanted to see him before I left.

After the session, the dozen officers and senior noncommissioned officers went to Colonel Ayers's home to have pizza and beer. His three young children, ranging in age from four to eight, pulled on his leg and vied for his attention all night. It was impossible not to sense the personal sacrifice he had made for his country again and again, and I was glad I didn't have young children to worry about during my own deployment, or a spouse waiting anxiously back home.

I left after an hour, much earlier than the other captains. I thanked Mrs. Ayers, and Colonel Ayers followed me out to my car. Like an older brother, he asked me how I was feeling and looked me in the eye. "Patrick," he said, "just take care of your troops and your commanders. You're going to be great."

•

The next morning, five of us paratroopers boarded a commercial plane from Fayetteville to Charlotte, and then another one to Washington, D.C. From there, we flew to London, where we had ten hours to see the city before our next commercial flight to Kuwait City. Three of the others were junior officers, fresh second lieutenants, one of whom was my former student at West Point and a newly minted Ranger. Another was Major Chris Eubank, a clean-cut signal officer who was a Virginia Military Institute graduate.

It was my first trip to London, and we made the most of our

last hours of freedom, taking a double-decker bus around the city, from Westminster Abbey to Buckingham Palace. Four of us also went to noon Mass, where I made my confession. After silently watching a strenuous political debate about Iraq between two men in Hyde Park, we went for a few beers. At the pub, we befriended some Brits, ended up ordering about ten pints and some shots of whiskey and tequila, and finally headed to Heathrow Airport after extending our self-imposed curfew. Although we tried unsuccessfully to get upgraded to business class, it didn't matter. We were out the whole flight and walked off the plane six and a half hours later, hurting from the heat and our hangovers.

After a couple days of training at Camp Champion in Kuwait, where I dropped what felt like several pounds in sweat, the five of us played the "Space-A-Shuffle," what soldiers call waiting with your gear at the airport, and finally climbed aboard the plane for the short afternoon flight into Baghdad. As we approached Baghdad International Airport, we began a rapid descent, making a gut-twisting corkscrew nosedive to evade enemy fire. Whatever anxiety I felt, I knew this would be one of the defining moments in my life. This was the moment I had been preparing for since 1993. This was why I had joined the army.

The Brass Ring

"So you're the newbies," remarked one of the paratroopers who had convoyed to Baghdad International Airport to pick us up. We nodded.

As we gathered our duffel bags, we were handed ceramic-plated Interceptor body armor (IBA) vests, an improvement over the Vietnam-era flak vests. When my travel companions were handed their weapons, I removed my rifle from its case and inserted a magazine of twenty 5.56-millimeter rounds. As the only one who had brought a rifle, I was suspected by another soldier of being a sniper whose identity as a JAG was a cover. Little did he know I hadn't even shot expert with my M4 rifle the week before.

Climbing into the second of two Humvees, we filled the metal benches that lined the back. Next to us was a stack of sandbags and a paratrooper holding a squad assault weapon

(SAW), which was larger than my M4 rifle. It was cramped, but there was just enough room by our feet to store our duffel bags. I pointed my rifle out in ready position. The paratrooper with the SAW warned us to look out for any Iraqi vehicles veering too close.

As the engine turned and we began our journey south, the tactical commander sitting in front made an announcement. Without even turning around to face us, he said, "Gentlemen, we're about to head down Route Irish, otherwise known as Ambush Alley. Lock and load." I chambered a round.

•

The war was still in its early stages, but the brigade I was joining was already legendary. The 2nd Brigade Combat Team of the 82nd Airborne Division, also known as the 325th Airborne Infantry Regiment, or the Falcon Brigade, had initially been assigned to jump into Baghdad Airport (then called Saddam Hussein International Airport) during the first nights of the invasion. But that mission was scrapped. They were needed elsewhere.

Because of the rapid success of our troops rolling up from the south, supply lines were being stretched thin. Support units, like the one that drew headlines when Private Jessica Lynch was captured, were getting hit and taking heavy casualties. As a result, the bulk of the 2nd Brigade was ordered to provide reinforcements. But when the order came for the brigade leadership to fly in, the air force grounded their plane, informing them that the flight was too risky. Captain Koby Langley later told me what broke the impasse. Apparently, the brigade commander, Colonel Arnold Bray, a man who embodied the army saying of "leading from the front," had walked up to the pilot of their C-130 and asked if he wanted to be the one who kept the 82nd from getting to the fight. He didn't. After they landed in total darkness on a small airfield under mortar fire, the 2nd Brigade fought their way north in Humvees, heroically clearing fedayeen insurgents in no less than twelve different cities before finally stopping in south central Baghdad in a district called Al Rashid.

•

Iraq's capital was divided into nine districts. Al Rashid, Baghdad's largest and poorest district, was west of the Tigris River and home to about 1.5 million Iraqis, about a quarter of the city's population. With its mixed Shia and Sunni population (there were no Kurds in our district), Al Rashid was literally and figuratively one of the hottest places on earth.

Our brigade was spread across Al Rashid, with smaller battalions and companies operating other small forward operating bases. Some FOBs had previously been schools; others were compounds formerly owned by Saddam. Each was austere, including ours, a warehouse off Ambush Alley that had been owned by the global truck manufacturer Scania. Hence its nickname: Scania. Otherwise, it was "the wire" because of the barbed wire that ran along its outer walls.

In the larger of the two buildings inside the wire, there was an open garage bay. But instead of broken trucks, the bay was now filled with dozens of green and olive drab canvas cots, lined up in rows about two feet apart, and sleeping more than a hundred members of the brigade staff, headquarters company, and military police platoon. Because the garage bay was crowded and hot, many troops went onto the rooftop to sleep at night. At first, this seemed sensible.

•

In the darkness of a midsummer night, about a dozen paratroopers and I raced up the stairs and onto our FOB's roof after hearing machine-gun shots fired. "Do you see the shooter?" I called out. "Anybody hit?" "No," someone yelled. In our haste up the stairs, most of us didn't have time to get our night-vision goggles. We crouched behind the three-foot-high lip of the roof, peering over the top and digging our chins into the concrete to shrink the size of our attacker's target. Instinctively flicking our weapons from safety to semiautomatic, we waited silently for a muzzle flash or tracer round to reveal our assailant's position, which we needed according to our rules of engagement (ROE) to fire back.

One soldier manned a hefty M60 machine gun and another a large M5 machine gun, enough firepower to take out a convoy of trucks. Suddenly, our M5 gunner's patience wore out. He unloaded a burst of five-inch rounds, firing aimlessly into the field where we all assumed the ghosts lay. He knew it wasn't ROE, but he couldn't help it. It was understandable, but not acceptable. We immediately ordered him to hold his fire. And then, quiet.

After that, we stopped sleeping on the roof.

•

The roof was only a couple of stories high. On each of the two floors there were several small offices. Covering the walls and tables inside were top-secret maps, standing orders like the rules of engagement, and large coffeemakers, among the other necessities of war. The largest office on the first floor became our brigade tactical operations center, or TOC, filled with folding tables, each belonging to a senior staff leader. The spotty electricity sometimes required us to work by flashlight even during the day because the windows were blocked by tall stacks of sandbags. When we were all packed inside, the smell of a dozen men who hadn't showered in a week could almost stop you in your tracks. But you got used to it.

The TOC was where our brigade conducted two top-secret daily battle update briefings (BUBs) at 7:00 a.m. and 7:00 p.m. These briefings were a time for each staff officer to brief the brigade commander and the brigade sergeant major on what had happened in the last twelve hours and what was likely to happen in the next twelve, providing what we called situational awareness within our battlespace.

The other small building, located in front near our only gate, headquartered our civil-military operations team. In this small complex, there was an office we could use to advise paratroopers on personal matters that required the privacy the TOC couldn't provide. There, paratroopers from FOBs across Al Rashid would spill their guts about problems back home, some legal and some personal, that had been gnawing at their hearts until they felt compelled to risk a convoy to Scania to get our advice.

When the brigade first arrived, they had to use filthy latrines, pouring diesel fuel into the basin and lighting it on fire to dispose of the waste, which smelled even worse than the trash that baked in the streets during the day. When we finally used one of the Iraqi Johnny on the Spot portable toilets, it wasn't a pleasant experience. The toilets baked in the sun and felt like saunas; our brown T-shirts under battle-dress-uniform (BDU) stuck to our chests with heavy sweat. Even worse were the swarms of flies and flying insects in the basin, which we felt crawling on our skin as we sat there, trying to do our business. Even so, the toilets were an improvement over the latrines.

With frequent bouts of diarrhea common and heat that hovered around 120 degrees—except for August, dubbed "fire month" by Iraqis and Americans, when it reached 138 degrees—

the army tried to keep us hydrated. We were each allocated two large one-liter water bottles a day. We'd bring one or two with us on convoys and share it. It was also with this rationed water that we shaved. Grabbing the side mirror of a parked Humvee, we poured the water into our canteen cups to rinse off our shavings from the blade. Between the brutal living conditions and the insistent unease, I don't think I ever fully adjusted to being in Iraq.

•

During my first few weeks in Baghdad, Captain Langley and I conducted a left-seat/right-seat training, where I spent a week watching how he did the job (left-seat training) and he spent a week watching me do the job (right-seat training). Like me, he had attended Catholic school, had a father who was a Democrat and a mother who was a Republican, and had helped pay his way through college with Army ROTC scholarships. We had both wanted to attend the University of Notre Dame, though I never applied, but I used to tease him that he took my spot in South Bend because there must have already been too many Irish Catholics named Murphy. He would jokingly shoot back, "Probably—there just weren't enough African-American Catholics like me!"

Captain Langley was an intense paratrooper, standing about 5'10" and a rock-solid 210 pounds, who shaved his head bald every other day. Although he got to the 82nd first, four years before me, he used to tease me—"I was only making sure that the brass ring was appropriately shined up for the Murph Dog!" The "brass ring" was the prize every judge advocate hungered for—the chance to prove yourself and protect your men on the field that matters most in the army: the field of battle.

The responsibility of leading such an outstanding group of

men was great, but I was able to draw on an education that had prepared me for my mission. I had learned many lessons over the years about leadership, some by trial and error, others by watching those around me. West Point itself had been an incubator of leadership. Throughout the years I studied the great American generals—Dwight Eisenhower, Norman Schwarzkopf, Douglas MacArthur, Colin Powell, Creighton Abrams, Barry McCaffrey—but there was one who stood out in my mind, so much so that I visited his gravesite in Luxembourg when I was stationed in Germany: General George S. Patton. He was a brilliant tactician, and an inspiration to his men, and I always remembered one of his key lessons on leadership:

> There's a great deal of talk about loyalty from the bottom to the top. Loyalty from the top down is even more necessary and is much less prevalent. One of the most frequently noted characteristics of great men who have remained great is loyalty to their subordinates.

I was determined to heed this guidance. As my brigade's judge advocate, I was succeeding Captain Langley as the leader of a Brigade Operational Law Team (BOLT), responsible for everything from advising commanders on targeting and combat operations, to prosecuting troops—if necessary—under the Uniform Code of Military Justice, to providing them with legal counsel when they unexpectedly received divorce or legal paperwork from home. Being a part of the only 82nd Airborne BOLT team now in Iraq was a privilege and a heavy responsibility—but one that each member of the team had spent years training for.

Our BOLT team was made up of six of the best paratroopers

in the U.S. Army. Drawn from different battalions, each a warrior first and a paralegal second. With these guys, any leader just needed to give direction; they had plenty of initiative and go get 'em attitude on their own. Most of the guys had nicknames. There was Specialist Shane "Mac" McKenney, a twenty-one-year-old from Florida. With his bleached-blond hair and stout frame, he looked just like a shorter version of Jon Gruden, the Tampa Bay Buccaneers football coach and former Eagles assistant coach. Mac always made sure he was taking care of his second battalion troops—known as the White Falcons. Partly because he was one of the more junior men in our BOLT, Mac would usually either drive one of our vehicles or be assigned as our gunner.

Specialist Juan "RV" Arevalo was a quick-witted and fearless twenty-year-old from Monte Alto, Texas, known for asking purposeful questions, like the time he turned to me during downtime and asked, "Sir, why are you a Catholic?" It was the kind of question that made you stop and consider what you had always taken for granted—a question that would have seemed out of place in civilian life, but all too reasonable at war. When it came to handing out intelligence and charm in heaven, we used to say, God sent RV back in line for seconds. He was a soldier's soldier, the best paratrooper I ever met. There wasn't a company commander or NCO on the brigade staff who didn't trust his word. We jokingly told the story of how RV had signed up for active duty in the army without even knowing that soldiers got paid. He had innocently thought the compensation was training, housing in the barracks, and free meals in the dining facility. Now that he was in Iraq, making $15,480 a year tax-free, he told everyone he was rich.

At night, around two or three in the morning, I'd often bring RV or one of the other guys on duty a cup of coffee or an Arabic-imprinted can of soda as they sat on their perch overlooking our compound, guarding the paratroopers sleeping below. Sometimes I'd also bring them a Snack Pack of chocolate pudding, a personal favorite that I had always had with Pop-Pop. Sharing them reminded me of home. Snack Packs and Tastykakes are Philadelphia traditions, manna from heaven for troops on the battlefield.

Sergeant J. R. "Three-Shot" Broussard was one of the three NCOs on our BOLT. A twenty-eight-year-old with sandy brown hair and a political science degree from Louisiana State University, Three-Shot grew up in Broussard, Louisiana, a town named after his great-great-grandpa. The nickname Three-Shot came that summer when he had been caught in a nasty hour-long firefight but managed to fire off just three shots. Three-Shot talked about finding a girlfriend almost as much as going to law school at LSU. With his easygoing nature and razor-sharp knowledge of the law, he led our civil-military operations and coordinated $4.5 million's worth of reconstruction projects—roughly one-third of the annual budget of Broussard, Louisiana.

Sergeant Sean Scarbough, nicknamed "Stick" for his thin frame, was the acting NCO in charge when I arrived. A big University of Notre Dame fan like Captain Langley and me, he also had a fiancée at home, one he worried would not be there on his return or after his next assignment to a special operations unit in Okinawa, Japan. He was also a practical joker, and his hearty laughs kicked up all the soot that a longtime cigarette addiction had put in his lungs. This guy bummed more smokes than anyone I'd ever seen, but he always made sure we were taking care of the commanders and troops from his first battalion, the Red Falcons.

Private First Class Juan "Santi" Santiago joined our team a few months after I arrived, replacing Stick. It was as if he'd been a member of our team for years. From Newport News, Virginia, he married young and had a wife, Latara, with two little sons back home, Angel and Alias. He had a rare and admirable combination of qualities: cool confidence, and the willingness to put in the hard work needed to get the job done. Only when you asked him could you see how he pined for his wife and kids. But he never complained.

The BOLT NCO in charge was Staff Sergeant Troy "Sarge" Robinson, a straitlaced soldier, on leave from Iraq when I arrived. Originally from Oklahoma, he was a devout Christian and had two children with his wife, Whitney. His baby boy, Ryan Patrick, was born several months into our tour, and it weighed on his heart that he couldn't be there for his son's birth. Sarge handled all the day-to-day responsibilities and kept the office humming. Before we'd set out on convoys, he was the one who checked to make sure our radio frequencies were correct and that our weapons were locked and loaded. He also got the latest intelligence on the routes we would be taking and what new tactics the insurgents were using, and he sometimes briefed our team before we left on a mission if I did not.

•

The night before Captain Langley left Iraq, our team got together to have cigars. It was a time to reflect, crack jokes, and say our good-byes. The next morning he left a note for me on our office computer, to be read after he was gone:

> You have many missions here Murph, and despite the sword and quill on your shoulders, a ton of them are going to be outside of that wire, so if you have to make a choice, sharpen the sword. The only mission that matters is ensuring that all the guys that left with you outside that wire, come back with you. If I thought for a second you could not do this, I would flex cuff you and toss you in the Euphrates, and stay here with my team. I know you are the right man. I have seen your heart, and we have broken bread in Communion. I thanked God that *you* were the one that stepped off of that C-130 to take over this mission. Find your strength with Him, and bring our guys back home alive Murph.

I promised him I would, and I did. Over the course of my tour, I led my BOLT team on over seventy-five missions around the city of Baghdad in support of our mission there. Every mission out and every mission in, we stayed a team, and all seven of us came back home. Nineteen men in our brigade wouldn't be as lucky.

Who Killed Specialist Keith?

At 2:01 a.m. on July 7, 2003, just a few days after I arrived in Iraq, I was awakened by Lieutenant Colonel Rowe, our brigade executive officer. “Murph, get up and report to the TOC. We have a KIA,” he whispered, placing his hand on my shoulder. An American soldier had been killed in action. I jumped up, dusted off my uniform, pulled on my desert boots, and hustled to the TOC.

There was a steady buzz of action reports coming in. Twenty-one-year-old specialist Chad L. Keith, from Batesville, Indiana, had been killed by a roadside bomb, also known as an improvised explosive device (IED). My BOLT team got to work drafting instructions on the mandated investigation into Specialist Keith’s cause of death. I also had to appoint a personal effects officer in Iraq, one back at Fort Bragg, and lastly, a paratrooper to return with the casket to the States.

After the facts were gathered and a briefing was held, someone said delicately, "The honeymoon is over, gentlemen." He was right. When Specialist Keith was killed, IEDs were a relatively new tactic. But they would soon become the leading cause of death of U.S. troops in Iraq, responsible for 70 percent of our casualties, including seven of the nineteen paratroopers in our brigade who were killed during my tour.

Improvised explosive devices are homemade bombs. In nearly any war zone, explosive materials can be found in a junkyard or bought on the black market. But in Iraq this was made exponentially worse because the Bush administration's disastrous planning had failed to secure sensitive sites. Toward the end of my tour, it was discovered that 380 tons of explosives were missing from a former Iraqi military facility that was supposed to be under U.S. control. That was enough munitions to arm insurgents for years and this was just one of over fifty unsecured sites with Iraqi munitions. Instead of citing the lack of boots on the ground or Iraqi incompetence for securing the site, former New York City mayor Rudy Giuliani blamed the troops when stumping for President Bush's close reelection in 2004. "No matter how you try to blame it on the president," he said, "the actual responsibility for it really would be for the troops that were there." Not to be outdone, former Tennessee senator Fred Thompson dismissed unsecuring the missing munitions as a "stupid thing."

But it wasn't just explosives that went missing. The U.S. Government Accounting Office has reported that in 2004 and 2005, 190,000 weapons, including 110,000 AK-47 machine guns, all paid for by U.S. taxpayers, went missing. Our military has no idea what happened to 30 percent of the weapons we distributed to Iraqi forces over the past several years. Back when I was a cadet, we used to chant, "I used to date a beauty queen. Now I date my M16." My fellow paratroopers could get court-martialed for losing their weapons, but the Bush administration had lost tons of explosives and thousands of weapons—arms that are no doubt now being used to maim and kill American troops.

To make matters worse, while the Bush administration's carelessness was helping arm our enemies, it was also undermining our ability to fight them. For starters, there was the body armor our soldiers wore. The *New York Times* has reported the details of a secret Pentagon study revealing that up to 80 percent of the marines killed in Iraq due to upper body wounds could have survived if they had been wearing additional body armor that the Pentagon had refused to provide them. Additionally, according to the study, thirty-one of the ninety-three fatal wounds came so close to the body armor that merely enlarging that armor "would have had the potential to alter the fatal outcome." The Pentagon declined to supply it for years.

We were also vulnerable in our Humvees. The army had been urged back in 1996 by its vehicle-program manager to move beyond the Humvee, calling it a Cold War relic with its twenty-five-year-old design. Humvees—with their flat hulls and frames that can only hold so much armor—are transport vehicles never intended for use in combat. They are extremely vulnerable to blasts from roadside bombs. And yet the army decided to make the Humvee the vehicle of choice in Iraq, no matter what the cost in human life and limb, because the Pentagon thought that relying on Humvees—as opposed to stronger, combat-ready vehicles—would be the fastest and least expensive option.

As a result, soldiers were left without up-armored vehicles. A month or so after Specialist Keith was killed, the Pentagon got around to ordering fifteen up-armored Humvees per month. Over a year and a half later, in December 2004, the need had still gone unaddressed. It's also come to light that in February 2005, commanders in Anbar Province, a hotbed of insurgency, filed an urgent request for Mine Resistant Ambush Protected (MRAP) vehicles. We "cannot continue to lose . . . serious and grave casualties to IED . . . at current rates when a commercial off the shelf capability exists to mitigate them," the request said. Nothing happened. Not long after I left Iraq, it was found that about half of the twenty thousand Humvees being used by the army had improvised shielding that still left the underside unprotected.

Many other Humvees were missing basic parts. The Humvee that my BOLT team used was actually missing doors during my tour. When we finally got doors later that fatal summer, after months of traveling unprotected up and down Ambush Alley, the makeshift steel doors didn't fit properly and didn't even have windows; apparently someone in Washington felt that doors were a luxury we could do without.

It was unconscionable. In 1942, when military planners came to President Roosevelt with their production goals for tanks, planes, and ships, FDR rejected their estimates, plugging in his own—far higher—numbers. The experts and authorities protested, saying it was simply impossible to meet the president's lofty goals. But Roosevelt waved them off, saying, "Oh, the production people can do it if they really try." He was right. Within just a few years, America was turning out annually 57,000 tanks, 109,000 airplanes, and 31,000 landing vessels. By contrast, when I left Iraq, there were just 6,000 fully protected vehicles in Iraq.

What was going on? According to the *New York Times*, the Pentagon's "procurement troubles had stemmed in part from miscalculations that underestimated the strength of the insurgency." But another reason for the delay became clear when Defense Secretary Donald Rumsfeld summarily dismissed the concerns of Specialist Thomas Wilson of the 278th Regimental Combat Team when the young soldier dared to challenge him during a question-and-answer session at Camp Buehring in Kuwait.

> Q: Why do we soldiers have to dig through local landfills for pieces of scrap metal and compromised ballistic glass to up-armor our vehicles?
>
> A: As you know, you have to go to war with the army you have, not the army you want. You can have all the armor in the world on a tank, and it can [still] be blown up.

The answer from the second-highest civilian military leader in our nation to one of the lowest-ranking enlisted soldiers in the army is now as infamous as the arrogance, and ineptitude, of the man who spoke it. This was the mind-set of the civilians running the war: Why give us armor if we might get killed, anyway?

•

We recognized the dangers of the relatively new IEDs. Leaving the wire meant preparing for battle. Even the most routine trip required traveling in a convoy of at least two vehicles, two or three men in each. As the captain and convoy tactical commander, I always rode shotgun in the lead vehicle with a radio attached to my ear, my right leg dangling out our doorless Humvee, my M4 pointed toward the ground, and my gunner on a SAW or an equally powerful .50-cal above in the turret. Each time we passed through the front gate, it felt like we were playing a game of Russian roulette.

On convoys, we drove fast and down the center of the road. IEDs were most commonly hidden along the roadside. Every twelve inches away from the curb, we were told, gave us another 10 percent chance of surviving a bomb blast. But even in the center lane, we weren't safe. In one of our daily intelligence briefs, we learned that an insurgent standing on an overpass had dropped an IED on a Humvee passing underneath. So we eyed every curb for bombs, every rooftop for snipers, every vehicle trying to get close—and now, every overpass.

On one patrol, baking in the sun, operating—as usual—on only a few hours of sleep, I strained my eyes, searching the landscape for any signs of danger. Then I heard the words that still make my heart race.

"Sir, I think I just saw an IED," RV said from the driver's seat next to me.

"What did it look like?" I yelled over the roar of the engine.

"It was a concrete cylinder-like thingy with wires sticking out."

Driving at fifty miles an hour, there was no way to be sure. But I trusted RV. So we radioed back to Scania, called for the bomb squad, gave them the six-digit grid coordinate of our location that I quickly plotted on my map (GPS was not standard issue), and told them we'd rendezvous just south at the site of the possible IED.

As we waited for the bomb squad to arrive, we initiated standard protocol when a possible IED was discovered—shutting down all six lanes of traffic in both directions, not an easy task for the handful of soldiers we had with us that day. It wasn't the best way to make friends with Iraqi commuters, who mostly grimaced at us behind their windshields, but it was a precaution that could save lives. That day, it did. The device RV caught was packed with two artillery shells, a force powerful enough to tear apart a couple of Humvees—killing about six people, if triggered at the right moment.

You learn in war—it becomes chiseled into your bones—that in most cases, there's no good reason why one person dies and another survives. It tears you apart when you start asking those questions, trying to make sense of the randomness of the violence and the killings. It reinforces your faith, or crushes it, or ignites a faith that was never there—as you hunger for an assurance that there is some reason for the chaos around you. The uncertainty of war—the uncertainty of my own survival—was often on my mind. I wrote in my journal on Thursday, July 31, 2003:

> About to go on a 2 vehicle convoy on the same road in which 3 ambushes occurred today. I'm a little afraid, but I refuse to back down. If I die, play Danny Boy, have J.J., Brian, Tony, Chris R., Norbeck and T.J. be my pallbearers, tell everyone to smile more often, have fun, and try to change the world (or someone's world), for the better every day, and tell Ashley that I thank her for teaching

> me what true, selfless love is, and that I expect her to move on, probably with a less charming, less muscular guy, but that I'll be waiting for her at the pearly gates and for that guy to expect some competition.

In Iraq, survival came down to a simple truth: Sometimes it's better to be lucky than good.

Hearts and Minds

Early that summer, there were leadership changes at the army, CENTCOM (Central Command), and our brigade—changes that were decided way above my pay grade and that came as a surprise to many of us on the ground. General Peter J. Schoomaker was persuaded to come out of retirement to be chief of staff for the U.S. Army. General John Abizaid was replacing General Tommy Franks as CENTCOM commander, overseeing our efforts in the Middle East. Last, Colonel Bray, our brigade commander, was being replaced by Colonel Kurt Fuller.

A former Oklahoma State wrestler, Colonel Fuller was a legend in the army. He was in his midforties and, like most officers in the 82nd, was an Airborne Ranger, with a rare yellow star above his paratrooper wings on his desert BDUs, signifying a combat jump, his earned in Grenada. When Colonel Fuller took over on Sunday, July 6, 2003, we all gathered in the TOC to hear him speak. We hung on every word uttered through his Oklahoma drawl and the tobacco in his mouth. As he spoke, I scribbled his words into my journal:

> Gentlemen, this is what I expect from you: Be a man. No sniveling. Know your job. Take care of your troops. And lead by example. My job is to make everyone in this brigade successful. So, every day you need to bring it. You need to bring your "A" game. You are doing a job that most Americans will not do. But right now they look up to and respect the military like no other time since WWII.

Colonel Fuller came as advertised. With his straight talk and sound judgment, he quickly earned our trust and loyalty. That night he called each officer on his brigade staff into his office to brief him on what we thought our jobs were, the status of what we were trying to accomplish, and what our priorities were going forward. I briefed him on my responsibilities and those of my BOLT team and described my professional philosophy: that I was his justice officer, and it was my job to ensure we followed the law. I told him that if I ever had concerns about an operation, as I sometimes would, I'd do my best to advise him on what we could legally do under the circumstances rather than to just say no. In addition, I said, my job was to take care of our soldiers by preventing legal matters back home like divorces from festering and creating morale problems here in Iraq.

And lastly, I told him, my job was to ensure that our BOLT team did everything we could to help win the hearts and minds of the Iraqi people.

•

Immediately after he took over, Colonel Fuller ordered us to be more aggressive with our Commander's Emergency Response Program (CERP) funds. These were discretionary funds that came from confiscated Iraqi money—including the $1.7 billion frozen in Saddam Hussein's personal funds—and were intended for reconstruction efforts, like refurbishing schools, police stations, and courthouses. Although the Bechtel Corporation was responsible for refurbishing dilapidated schools within our district, we soon found that their Iraqi subcontractors had done embarrassingly shoddy work. So we decided that every project had to have two competitive estimates before a bid was given.

One of our BOLT team's early initiatives was providing electricity and air-conditioning for the main courthouse in our district. We also hired day laborers to clean up the streets in Al Rashid. It was a custom in Iraq to dump trash into abandoned lots, but that posed a number of risks. Trash heaps could generate threats to public health and also were good places to hide IEDs. So sanitation was in everyone's interest. It was initially frustrating because trash dumping would resume as soon as we cleaned it up, but we discovered that if we turned a dumping ground into a soccer field, residents would seldom use it as a trash lot again. We also contracted to purchase soccer balls for Iraqi children. Seeing their faces light up made even the toughest paratrooper smile.

While our civil-military operation officers took the lead on this, I was responsible for ensuring that every request up to $50,000 was spent properly and not being used to benefit coalition forces or entertain local Iraqis or support individual businesses. Our paratroopers were extremely aggressive in implementing this program, and each night I'd have a stack of requests on my folding table in the TOC. We always turned them around the same day, and by the end of our tour, we had spent over $4.5 million in

CERP funds to help rebuild Al Rashid. It may only have been a drop in the bucket, but it was a start.

•

The day Colonel Fuller took over was also the day Captain Langley and our team paid the first foreign claim in Iraq. At the inception of the war, the civilian brains in Washington had assumed that since Iraq was a combat zone, wartime damage would be the responsibility of the Iraqis, not the United States. Following traditional military doctrine, the United States does not pay for property damages or wrongful deaths that result from combat operations. But under the Foreign Claims Act, a law initiated by President Roosevelt during World War II, the United States can pay in cases where U.S. troops are found to be negligent. So the minute President Bush declared major combat operations over while speaking on the deck of the USS *Abraham Lincoln* shortly before I deployed, the United States started receiving claims of negligence.

As the United States shifted from being a liberator to being an occupier with the speedy overthrow of Saddam Hussein, our policies had to shift as well. Commanders were beleaguered by Iraqi civilians pressing at the gates of compounds demanding redress for homes that had been destroyed or loved ones who had been killed. There were more claims each passing week as the situation in Iraq continued to deteriorate. Combat deaths, both military and civilian, were on the rise, and the seeds of the insurgency were being sown, just as our enemy had planned. Although casually dismissed by Donald Rumsfeld in June 2003 as "dead-enders," the insurgency had in fact been planned by Saddam Hussein before his ouster, a fact confirmed by our 82nd commanding general.

Initially, the claims mission was not the army's to carry out. The plan was for the air force to handle claims once all combat operations were over, but, for the most part, air force personnel weren't conducting ground combat missions and weren't in cities across Iraq like the army and marines were. So tasking the air force with that assignment didn't make a lot of sense, as was quickly becoming clear to commanders on the ground.

Before I arrived in Iraq, Captain Langley and the BOLT team had received their marching orders from an exasperated Colonel Bray. "Gentlemen, I don't care *what* anyone is saying about why we can't do it—my mission here is failing without a way to help these folks. This part of the war is *your* part—*get it done!*" Captain Langley and the team forced the army and military bureaucracy to act. Within a few weeks, the CENTCOM commander and the United States Army Claims Service (USARCS) at Fort Meade, Maryland, pulled the assignment from the air force. It was one of our many tasks now, and the Army JAG Corps was, as always, ready to flex for the mission.

•

Despite the overwhelming odds, our BOLT team partnered with a local Iraqi attorney, Mohammed Zamel, and the Iraqi judges at the local courthouse to set up a system to compensate Iraqi civilians. Captain Langley, RV, Mac, Stick, and I jumped into our doorless Humvee, the lead vehicle in our convoy. We had traded favors for an armed military police escort, affectionately referred to as Paratrooper Death Dealers, to drive us to the Al Bayaa courthouse—a quasi-operational court in Iraq in the heart of southern Baghdad. To help restore confidence in the judicial system, we chose to pay these Iraqi claims at the local courthouse, not at our FOB, which would have been much safer for us. We left the wire armed with weapons and all the paperwork we'd need for our first claims mission.

But before we went to the court, we had another stop to make. We headed to the finance officer's meager compound at an FOB just south of ours. When we got there, we handed him about two dozen vouchers for cash. He looked at us like we were crazy. "Let me get this straight, the brigade commander wants you to drive into the center of Baghdad with a bag full of cash and start handing it out to Iraqis?" Captain Langley nodded—"It's our mission." He couldn't believe it. "Whatever, man, it's your funeral. I got the paperwork I need, you're good to go." We strolled out of the office with a few thousand dollars in U.S. currency in a brown paper bag—all small bills. Then we jumped into the Humvee, RV driving, Mac as the gunner, Stick and I in the back, and Captain Langley riding in front for the last time before he redeployed back home.

No one had seen, or heard of, anything like this in all of Iraq. We were paying Iraqis for our own negligent acts. Public sentiment was on the steady decline, and the commanders sensed it. Setting up a claims system was just a finger in the dam—our finger—but we weren't going to be deterred. The drive to the courthouse was long and dusty, and we took an alternate route in case one of the Iraqi interpreters "accidentally" mentioned the mission to a friend. At that point, we weren't sure whom we could trust, not even the Iraqis who asked for our help each day, and we continually scanned the buildings for threats.

By the time we reached the courthouse, the Iraqis receiving payment had already been notified where to find us. Word was spreading that "millions" of American dollars were being doled out; this kind of distortion of the facts was the norm in Iraq. We jumped out of our Humvee, moved though the growing throngs of Iraqis, and climbed the stairs of the courthouse, straining our necks to peer up the stairwell for any sign of danger. When we got to the third floor, where the president of the Al Bayaa court's office was located, it was well lit and generally cool—thanks to the industrial generator we had recently provided with CERP money. The MPs pulled security outside the courthouse.

When we got inside, the court president thanked us, and asked us to sit for tea. RV looked at me and shook his head. He was right, of course—we had to get this mission done right, done quick, and then get the hell out of there. But it was considered insulting not to accept such an offer, so we sat down and tried to enjoy it, drinking the hot, sugary tea as fast as we respectfully could.

While the military police patrolled the crowd outside, my team secured the third floor, with Stick as the gunner taking a spot in the corner from an open window to the rear of our table. As the first Iraqi claimant approached, trying to look around RV, who was guarding the door, I called his name, and RV let him pass. Captain Langley had him fill out the paperwork and sign his name for our records. The transaction took less than a minute; I believe it was no more than twenty dollars. The Iraqi gentleman thanked us profusely, and the interpreter said it was enough to feed his family for a month. "I Love Airborne, I Love Airborne, I Love Airborne!" he shouted as he ran back down the hallway. It may have been the only English he knew, but it was more than enough to make us all smile.

I looked over at Stick, who was standing by the window, scanning the crowd in the streets below. Captain Langley commented to him with a chuckle, "One heart and mind down, buddy, hang in there!" Stick replied, stone-faced, "That's great, sir, let's just get the hell out of here. They can keep their hearts and minds. I want to keep my head from being splattered across this wall."

•

Some of the claims filed with our team were no more than a few paragraphs scribbled on cardboard, but each had to be treated with care. Even the vaguest hint of indifference on our part could incite a desperate Iraqi. At first, some war-weary paratroopers who didn't have the necessary sensitivity required for these tasks were kept away. When I asked one of my men about the Iraqis at the front gate of Scania, he told me frankly, "I just tell them to get lost—that's probably why they don't let me meet Iraqis outside the gate."

In the beginning, it wasn't clear to a couple members of our team why it was so important to win the Iraqis' hearts and minds. We had to convince them that this new claims process was just as important as our other legal tasks, like criminal prosecution, training the new Iraqi Army, and providing legal assistance to our paratroopers. We needed the buy-in of every paratrooper in our BOLT team, and within a few weeks, even the couple of paratroopers who had been hesitant came around.

Soon I tasked Mac to lead our claims effort. He worked with Attorney Zamel to ensure that each claim met two benchmarks: proven negligence confirmed by sworn witness statements describing how the damage occurred; and estimated damages, usually obtained through two sets of estimates. It was my job to decide which claims arose from coalition forces' negligence and which arose due to collateral damage from combat—that is, which we should pay and which we should reject. This was often an absurd distinction. How do you tell what damage is caused by negligence and what is caused due to combat when you're at war? The whole country was a combat zone. But it was a distinction the Foreign Claims Act required us to make, so we took it seriously.

That early in the war, we were the only office in Iraq paying claims, so claims poured in from all over Baghdad by the hundreds. We had to train nine other Iraqi attorneys just to help us investigate and adjudicate our ballooning workload, and we joked that that we had unleashed personal injury lawyers all across Baghdad. The claims covered the whole spectrum of war damage—from loss of life to looting, from stolen possessions to destroyed homes. There was an Iraqi who claimed that one of our Humvees, wider than some of Baghdad's narrow lanes, had clipped a side of his taxi, causing obvious damage. "How am I going to make a living?" he asked one of our paratroopers at the gate. "Use the other side," was the instant reply. Not helpful.

One Iraqi even came in alleging a tank had run over his car. The 82nd didn't have any armored tanks; we are light infantry. But pictures, witness statements, and an apology note from a 1st Armored Division soldier persuaded me. I'm not sure if car damage from a tank has a parallel in the civilian world, the requisite legal standard to treat it as noncombat damage. But where I come from, car damage is car damage, so as the adjudicator, I paid the claim. Other times, Iraqis would file claims charging that paratrooper engineers detonating controlled explosions of confiscated illegal Iraqi ammunition had accidentally damaged their homes. I usually paid those, too.

More than once, Iraqis claimed that in the middle of the night, paratroopers had jumped through their windows or kicked down their doors or damaged their homes with a concussion grenade. I'd confirm the date and check with our battalion commands to make sure that these Iraqis weren't lying. It was common for paratroopers—the men who took out our most lethal enemies—to assault a house using these tactics. Occasionally, we would discover that as a result of poor intelligence or the fact that buildings in Baghdad aren't well marked with street addresses, they had assaulted the wrong home, leaving amid the damage a note of apology instructing them to "see CPT Murphy at Scania." Some may conclude that knocking someone's door down during a raid is a combat activity and argue that I shouldn't have paid these claims. But while I was doing my best to interpret the army regulation and help establish a rule of law in a city that hadn't had one for decades, I also felt that by paying some of these claims we were making it less likely that an angry Iraqi would join the insurgency. So I was proud to pay claims I reasonably could.

One man repeatedly appeared at our compound and the courthouse with his daughter. She was maybe thirteen years old, her skin grotesquely scarred with deep-tissue burns from her neck down to her belly button. Meeting with them one day, I looked shyly at the Polaroids he'd taken of her deformed chest, embarrassed that I had somehow transgressed this young girl's privacy merely by glancing at the photos. When he offered to lift up her shirt to show me in person, I said no.

I had no evidence that U.S. forces had caused the injury, as the girl's father alleged; but whoever was responsible, we had to help. Week after week, he and his daughter returned. Finally, with Colonel Fuller's approval, I offered her family *solatia*, a token of sympathy, equivalent to $1,000, different from a formal payment for damages under the Foreign Claims Act. These *solatia* payments were not an admittance of guilt, but an expression of sympathy. The amount was several times her father's annual salary and the maximum we could give for personal injuries. It was a small consolation for what would be a lifetime of suffering.

Not everyone was satisfied with what they were paid. "My car was damaged and my left eye was hurt by flying glass," said one Iraqi named Assim, who was caught in the middle of a firefight with insurgents. "What's five hundred American dollars?!" His reaction was common. But overall, I believe the Iraqis were happy that justice—however imperfect—was finally being delivered. Certainly not every claim was payable. But usually, even when they were denied, the Iraqis would appreciate the fact that we had taken the time to listen to them—a far cry from the practices of Saddam's regime.

•

Eventually, we had to narrow our parameters and accept claims that came only from within the Al Rashid district, rather than all nine districts in Baghdad. We were also tasked with advising other BOLT teams across Iraq on how to implement our system. By the time I left Iraq, we had received thousands of claims, transferring some to other BOLT teams, adjudicating more than 1,600. I denied more than 1,300 claims. Eighteen percent of the time, I found U.S. forces negligent and paid the Iraqi claimant, awards totaling $203,705, with the average award around $650 per Iraqi. Two hundred thousand U.S. dollars may not sound like a lot, but it equaled nearly $100 million in the Iraqi economy.

The team had achieved the impossible, defying the policy void and red tape that stood in the way. Our model would become the backbone of what is now a more than $30 million foreign claims system in Iraq and widely recognized as an example of how the United States can help achieve stability through goodwill.

The Golden Rule

July 3, 2003, was a special day for our team.

We had to convoy to the Baghdad International Airport, about twelve miles from our base, to resolve some legal matters, and had two other nonofficial stops to make while we were there. The first stop was for our guys, who for months had eaten the dreaded meals ready to eat (MREs)—"meals rejected by the enemy," we had called them in training—that had left them yearning for a Whopper. And today, the first Burger King in Iraq was opening at the airport.

The other stop was to see Ashley, who was stationed at the airport as a combat engineer. When I landed in Iraq a few days earlier, I was carrying in my pocket a diamond engagement ring; it felt like it was burning a hole through my pocket. I had been saving money from my $46,000-a-year salary and had asked her father for her hand in marriage. Ashley had already been in Iraq for months and was redeploying home in a couple of weeks. This was my chance. As we pulled into the airport, our team arranged to regroup forty-five minutes later. Within ten minutes, I found Ashley's engineer battalion. Then I saw her. Her blond hair was shorter now, just below her ears; when I had last seen her, she had hair down below her shoulders. She looked beautiful.

After briefly catching up, I suddenly bent down on one knee and asked her to marry me. She said yes and we consummated it with a kiss. Soon my BOLT team and her fellow Texan RV returned to say it was time to go. I would see her briefly one more time before she redeployed to Germany and then to her new assignment at Fort Bragg with the XVIII Airborne Corps. I told her not to worry—we had all heard rumors that we'd be back at Fort Bragg by Labor Day.

•

By late summer, tensions were running high in the 82nd. Rumors of when we would return home were rampant. We had seen other units leave and most of us hoped it would be our turn soon. The distance hurt. To help keep morale strong in our team, I wrote to their families with updates. I would never write about the dangers we faced, just the great job their paratroopers were doing. RV confided in me one night that his mother didn't read English very well, and while his little sister did, his mom was never sure if the letter would be good news or bad, so she always had a family friend translate it for her first. He was her only son, and she prayed the rosary every day that one day he'd return home to Texas.

I also tried to call my own parents once a month from our satellite phone, and wrote as often as possible, sometimes sending up to three letters a week; e-mail was usually unavailable or unreliable. Receiving care packages from family and friends was a special event, and my team knew that what was mine was theirs. Even clipped articles about my beloved Philadelphia sports teams—the Phillies, Eagles, Sixers, or Flyers—would make me feel connected to home. My sister, brother, and mom wrote twice a month or so, sometimes just a quick postcard, sometimes long three-page letters describing life back home. My father wrote the most. He'd send four letters a week, usually on the same photocopied letterhead with the Murphy family crest, keeping his remarks to a page, and always ending with "Love Always, Dad."

In August, when my mother wasn't home for my call, I told my dad I thought we were getting extended again, and that I definitely would not be back by Labor Day and probably not for Thanksgiving, or even Christmas. I could tell his heart was in his throat and tried to comfort him; I asked him not to tell Mom or Ashley.

•

One midsummer night, sitting in our TOC, writing a note to my college hockey teammate Bano and his wife, thanking them for their care packages, I heard a noise and dropped my pen. It was the whistle of incoming mortar rounds, and their explosion by our compound. The sounds were getting louder and louder as the insurgents adjusted their aim—inching their mortars closer and closer. A deadly game of trial and error.

It was one of the times in Iraq that I felt true fear. I was convinced that our thin concrete wall would crash into us. I could run to another part of the TOC, even another part of Scania, but there was no way of knowing where the mortar would land. I was convinced this was it. I hunkered on one knee, gripping my fist, trying to look strong like the time years earlier during airborne school when I hid my fear as I was about to jump out of an airplane. I thought about what I could do to protect my head so that even if I lost my arms or legs, I could still look at the world without the scowl of a mangled face. But there was no bunker I could crawl into. No vest or helmet that could fully protect me against a blast. All that could save me now was prayer. So I prayed.

The insurgents got off five mortar shots in four endless minutes, as I listened for the screams of any injured paratroopers. It took our radar five minutes to track their position so our artillerymen could launch counterfire. (All too often, the insurgents attacked us from a residential neighborhood, expecting that when we fired back, we might hurt civilians.) Finally, the mortaring stopped, and I returned to the letter I had been drafting, still trembling from what had happened. It wasn't the first time we had been mortared while I was writing Bano and his wife, and I couldn't help myself: "I love you guys," I wrote, "but it seems like whenever I write you, we get mortared so no offense, but this is the last time I'm sending you any letters." I smiled inside, thinking my buddy must be a curse. No wonder our hockey record at King's was so bad.

•

The strain of extended tours had some units complaining to the press. Colonel Fuller would have none of it. He let it be known rather bluntly at the evening BUB that we had a task to do, and that we'd go home when the president told us it was time. We still needed to capture high-value target number one, Saddam Hussein. "Plan to be here until 2004," he said. Our chaplain put it differently. "God has something for us to do here," he said. "He'll watch out for us and send us home when He's ready."

My fellow paratroopers coped with the strain in different ways. It didn't help that we were all ordered to take antimalaria pills. Our army doctor warned us the pills would play with our moods, making us a little "agitated" or causing us to have "vivid dreams." They did. To release frustration, some paratroopers started lifting, using left-behind truck axles at Scania as weights.

Others wrote home with greater frequency, and most tried to make light of the situation. When we had intelligence in midsummer that our compound would be attacked on July 17, the thirty-fifth anniversary of the 1968 Baath Party Revolution, our headquarters company commander commented dryly at the evening BUB, "In recognition of the Iraqi holiday, we're going to put some extra guards up on the roof."

Unfortunately, a few paratroopers turned to illegal drugs like hashish and Valium, which were readily available on the streets we patrolled. No one likes prosecuting their own, but a vital part of our BOLT team was to ensure that military justice was being enforced. Colonel Fuller had a no-bullshit attitude when it came to discipline. He was tough but fair. When paratroopers acted up, which they did, whether it was talking back to an NCO or drinking beer bought from an Iraqi (alcohol, sex, pornography, and drugs were illegal for soldiers on deployment), justice was swift.

Most times, when verbal or written counseling wouldn't cut it as punishment, nonjudicial punishment was ordered, known as an Article 15. There were different levels of punishment based on rank, but for lower-ranking troops, like a private first class or specialist, they usually involved being demoted to private, losing pay, and being assigned extra duty for several weeks. Paratroopers could seek legal counsel, which meant convoying them to the Baghdad Airport, where two defense attorneys were stationed.

Each paratrooper could also turn down the Article 15 and demand a trial by court-martial. My BOLT team helped commanders implement over a hundred Article 15s and eighteen courts-martial in my time in Iraq.

Because a full trial at a "general" court-martial was time-consuming—requiring a military judge to fly into Iraq—our brigade often used "summary court-martial," a trial where the judge could be one of our higher-ranking field grade officers, usually a battalion commander with the rank of lieutenant colonel, one rank below Colonel Fuller. At summary courts-martial, the maximum punishment could be jail for thirty days for lower enlisted troops, while there was no such punishment for higher ranks unless a general court-martial was ordered.

•

As 120 paratroopers returned to their small FOB in a closed-down school, weary from a 1:00 a.m. mission, almost all of them hit their cots for some much-deserved sleep. Two paratroopers were tasked to stand guard on the roof on the first rotation, providing security while their brothers-in-arms slept below. Instead of drinking coffee or soda, chewing gum, or sharing stories to stay awake and alert, they took out small pills sold to them illegally by a local Iraqi that they understood to be Valium. Moments later they fell unconscious, directly compromising the safety of their fellow paratroopers. These paratroopers were so out of it—their lifeless bodies not moving even when repeatedly shaken—that their replacements at first thought they were dead.

Regardless, a message had to be sent. I advised Colonel Fuller, and he ordered a summary court-martial for both. Each received the maximum thirty days in jail, becoming the first

U.S. soldiers to be confined as the result of a court-martial at Camp Arifjan, a $200 million state-of-the-art facility in Kuwait. After being demoted to private, losing two-thirds pay for one month, and being released from jail, they were sent back to Fort Bragg, North Carolina, where they were chaptered out of the army without an honorable discharge. Tough, but fair.

•

In the aftermath of our invasion, Secretary of Defense Donald Rumsfeld had dismissed the wide-scale looting by saying "stuff happens" and freedom is "untidy." Meanwhile, our soldiers were trying to stop it. Some went too far. One lieutenant in Baghdad came across a looter, ordered his men to flex-cuff him, and loaded him onto the back of his truck. Driving miles from the Baghdad neighborhood where the man had been apprehended, the lieutenant stopped the truck in an open field at dusk, dragged out his captive, and forced him to kneel in front of his idling vehicle, under the bright glare of its front lights, in full view of his soldiers.

The lieutenant then drew his weapon, a nine-millimeter Beretta pistol, put it to the Iraqi's head, said something to him, and fired into the air, terrifying the man, who began sobbing uncontrollably. The lieutenant climbed into his front seat and drove off, leaving the Iraqi, still bound by flex cuffs and shivering in fear, crying in the fetal position in a field, miles from home.

A few days later, two sergeants in the 82nd, under the temporary command of this same sadistic lieutenant and present during this earlier episode, came across a copper factory being looted by an Iraqi and his two teenage sons. Caught in the act, their car full of copper, they were apprehended as the father pleaded with the soldiers, explaining that he was merely trying to feed his starving family.

The sergeants radioed back to their lieutenant, communicating the father's explanation, and asking what to do next. "Set them free," the lieutenant instructed, "but not before you make them cry." The sergeants, having seen their lieutenant's behavior in the field, knew just what he meant. They approached the father with an Iraqi translator: "Tell him, we're going to punish you for your crimes—which son do you want to die?" As the words were translated, the father pleaded with them in Arabic: "Pick me. Please, pick me." The sergeant repeated his question, and it was translated again. The father wept. "Pick me," he begged.

One sergeant grabbed the younger of the two sons, a boy not older than twelve, and took him out of the father's sight behind the factory. There, the sergeant fired his M4 into the air. The boy's father cried out, assuming his son had just been gunned down. Moments later, the sergeants reappeared with the son, physically unharmed, and told the father and his boys to "get the fuck out of here."

When Colonel Fuller learned about this, he came directly to me. "Murph," he said, "we can't have this happening." I advised Colonel Fuller that, since a regular court-martial would take months, we should initiate a summary court-martial for the sergeants. Their ranks of sergeant would save them from jail time, but not from being expelled from the army without an honorable discharge, a stain on their service that would trail them for the rest of their lives.

I really wanted to go after the lieutenant; these two sergeants were just following his criminal lead. The army should make an example out of him, I urged the lieutenant's command at the Baghdad Airport. But, unlike the two sergeants, the lieutenant was not in the 82nd, so we didn't have authority to prosecute him. Further, the lieutenant's commanding officer thought the evidence was poor. I agreed that it wouldn't be an easy trial victory, but I felt we should not limit our trials to those cases we were certain to win—we should take on important, symbolic cases in the interest of justice, even if there were risks of acquittal. I lost the argument. Ultimately, the lieutenant resigned, the sergeants were given a summary court-martial, and the incident was lost in the fog of war.

•

One of our BOLT team's additional responsibilities was to ensure that troops understood and enforced laws governing the proper treatment of detainees. "Treat them with dignity and respect, don't lavish them with luxury," I'd repeat as if it were a mantra. "You don't have to give them hot food or a radio, but be sure they have three MREs, water, and clean water basins to wash their faces."

To help our troops understand what was expected of them, we prepared a checklist of what each detainee was entitled to have in a cell. In November, I added a heater to the checklist. After suffering through the 138-degree heat of August, it felt like West Point winters when the temperature hit the thirties. I was looking out for the human rights of our detainees, but I was also trying to look out for Colonel Fuller. If one of our detainees had come down with pneumonia or died on our watch, even in those pre–Abu Ghraib days, it would have been all over CNN, and our brigade would—justifiably—have faced severe criticism.

Every few weeks, our BOLT team visited at least one of the

other FOBs in our sector to inspect their detainee cells to make sure they had all the items on our checklist. "You get what you measure," I'd counsel our team, urging them to ensure compliance with our rules. Most paratroopers readily complied. But a major at our own FOB kept dragging his feet. When I reminded him repeatedly that a heater was required in each cell, his answer was always, "Yeah, yeah, yeah"—and nothing got done.

One day, during a briefing in the TOC, our army doctor reinforced the need for heaters in the cells. As soon as the briefing was over, I went up to the major who had been ignoring my guidance. Even though he was a higher-ranking officer, I gave it to him straight. "Sir, I told you, we need heaters. Have one in those cells tonight!" "Don't tell me how to do my job," he shot back, motioning to take our conversation outside. My temper was rising. "I wouldn't have to, if you did your damn job." I thought one of us was about to throw a punch. Thankfully, it didn't come to that and, a short time later, a heater was placed in each cell.

•

My view on the treatment of detainees went back to something I learned as a child at St. Anselm's Elementary School. "So in everything," Jesus said in his Sermon on the Mount, "do to others what you would have them do to you, for this sums up the Law of the Prophets." It's known as the Golden Rule, and it's not always easy to follow in war.

In combat, when your brothers and sisters in arms are being wounded and maimed and killed every day, it's not easy to show compassion and mercy to those who are responsible. It's not easy to take a step back and recognize that vengeance is in no one's interest. It's not easy. But it's necessary.

There's a reason we have laws of war. There's a reason we spend so much time teaching those laws at West Point and throughout military training. It's not just that treating other human beings decently, even in war, is worth doing in and of itself. It's that there are strategic consequences when we don't treat our enemies with mercy and compassion.

On the first day of Operation Desert Storm in 1991, tens of thousands of Iraqis in Kuwait held up makeshift white flags, even under threat of execution from Saddam, because they knew that Americans would treat them with dignity and that we would return them to their families when the conflict was over. Members of the military profession have time-honored traditions that we cannot throw away because of an enemy who does not respect the laws of war. We are guided by principles. They define who we are. And when we compromise them, we're inflicting a wound on ourselves that's more damaging than any enemy attack.

Fridays in Never-Never Land

Every Friday, we assembled a convoy of two or three vehicles and drove to the Coalition Provisional Authority's (CPA) Ministry of Justice in the Green Zone, a collection of Saddam's most spacious and ostentatious palaces that now houses the American Embassy—the largest foreign embassy in the world. The purpose of these trips was to attend meetings with the top military and civilian leaders responsible for Iraq's fledgling legal system.

Although one of our paratroopers always guarded our vehicles until he was relieved, I didn't want the others to have to sit in the hall while I attended the meetings. So I'd order them to eat a hot meal at the palace's cafeteria and conduct "water survival training" in the palace pool—an order that meant, in effect, go for a swim—a welcome treat, especially before we got shower stalls at Scania.

The thirty senior military lawyers at the meeting included British officers who would fly to Baghdad by helicopter from Basra in the south, the 101st Airborne soldiers coming in from Mosul in the north, and some marines from Al Anbar in the west. All but three of the people around that table outranked me and most were about twenty years older. But I had a seat at the table because our district had two of the fourteen courthouses in Baghdad, along with twenty-five judges.

En route to the Green Zone, we'd first travel north and stop at the Baghdad Airport, navigating through its heavily fortressed perimeter to pick up Colonel Sharon Riley, the staff judge advocate for Lieutenant General Martin Dempsey, division commander of the 1st Armored Division, the same unit I was assigned to back in Germany in 1998. She was sharp and hard-charging, and her NCO, Master Sergeant Brian Quorum, was one of the most affable, lighthearted, and talented NCOs I ever met. One day he pulled my men and me aside and thanked us for the weekly convoys. He knew the risks of traveling up and down Ambush Alley and said with a smile, "We always feel safer rollin' with the eighty-deuce boys." It made our paratroopers proud. His only shortcoming was that he thought his previous military unit, the 101st Airborne Division, was better than the 82nd.

•

Our BOLT team missed only one Friday meeting during my tour in Iraq. It happened in the fall as we were traveling to pick up Colonel Riley at the airport and found an Iraqi man lying facedown in the middle of the road. Even in Baghdad, that wasn't something we saw every day. It was a side road, only two lanes, but no one was around. It wasn't clear whether he was alive or dead. But with recent intelligence reports that insurgents were placing roadside bombs inside animal carcasses and human bodies, it occurred to me that the body could be wired with explosives. So I wasn't about to let my men take any unnecessary chances.

With our team and a military police escort providing 360-degree security, I slowly approached the body from about ten feet away. My heart was racing but I couldn't see any blood. He was wearing only one sandal, which signified to me that he must not have just passed out there. I lay down on the ground at his level, looking for any signs of breathing. There were none. The body remained eerily still. Then I noticed what looked like multiple gunshot wounds on the side of his chest. We called for Iraqi police backup, which as usual was unreliable and took over thirty minutes to arrive. To the best of my knowledge, his death remained a mystery and his identity was never confirmed—in all likelihood, another civilian caught in the crosshairs of this war.

Estimates vary wildly on the number of Iraqi civilians who have been killed since the start of the U.S. invasion. In 2006, the *Los Angeles Times* stated that "at least 50,000 Iraqis have died violently since the 2003 U.S.-led invasion." Others put the number significantly higher. Numbers like that can easily become abstractions. We can forget that each digit represents human beings with hopes and dreams and families who loved them—a son or daughter, brother or sister, mother or father, who left home one day and never returned. At the very moment, I was staring down at that man in the street, somewhere in Baghdad, his absence was tearing a family apart.

●

Back in the Green Zone, those Friday meetings provided a window into the dysfunction at the heart of the Coalition Provisional Authority (CPA)—its lack of manpower, lack of urgency, and lack of understanding of what was happening on the ground. A typical example concerned weapons cards, or gun permits. After the U.S. invasion, the Bush administration decided not to disarm the country, violating one of the fundamental rules of military occupation. Instead, they decided to permit each household to own one AK-47 machine gun and fifty rounds of ammunition. Yet, while the Iraqi population was armed to the teeth, our judges and translators—who put their lives on the line each day for Iraq, America, and our troops—were not legally permitted to carry weapons.

Unlike in America, laws in Iraq become effective when they are posted in courthouses. But the CPA didn't bother to adhere to this Iraqi custom, and after the CPA issued laws we were not even given copies of the new laws to distribute to our judges and post in our courthouses. So the new CPA laws often remained essentially null and void, leaving each district in Iraq to follow its own procedures.

At our Friday meetings, many of us asked for Arabic copies of the new CPA laws and were told, "We're working on it." Week after week for about six weeks, I continued to get the same response. Finally, after losing credibility with my district's judges, I had enough. "I've been asking for these CPA orders for six weeks!" I shouted at the next meeting. "Someone needs to start acting with a sense of urgency around here. I could have had a paratrooper flown to the U.S., parachute into Kinko's, and do this in a week. Let's get it done!"

It was an unexpected outburst, but one that was long overdue. Something needed to be said. "We'll have it on the Web site tomorrow," offered one of the civilian leaders in the room. "With all due respect, sir," I fired back, "there's limited electricity and no Internet in my courthouses. Getting it on the Web site won't cut it." Chewing out our civilian leadership was not condoned. But it was completely unacceptable for my men to travel up Ambush Alley every Friday when all I got was a "we're working on it." Too many soldiers and civilians in the Green Zone—in this palace—just didn't get it. They seemed to live in a different country, isolated from the reality of Iraq. They had three hot meals a day, showers, movie night, a pool, and air-conditioning. At Scania, we had guard duty and MREs.

As a result of their failures to act, the 82nd continued taking matters into our own hands. We printed and distributed weapons cards ourselves, issuing to our judges and interpreters weapons that we had seized from insurgents. It was the only way to get the job done. During one raid, I went one step further, "appropriating" for our translator Alyaa a confiscated pistol, which Mac taught her to use.

•

Printing weapons cards wasn't the only area in which we had to take matters into our own hands because of inefficient civilian leadership. One of our other duties was to help foreign-born paratroopers who wanted to become U.S. citizens. Paratroopers would convoy in two or three vehicles from their FOBs throughout Al Rashid to our Scania FOB, taking time from patrols or from simply resting on their cots to get our help. I'd tell them what forms they had to fill out and assure them that I'd follow up with the relevant agent from the U.S. Customs and Immigration Service (USCIS), the agency called the Immigration and Naturalization Service (INS) before being submerged within the Department of Homeland Security (DHS).

A year before I got to Iraq, President Bush had signed Executive Order 13269, eliminating the three-year service requirement for active-duty soldiers seeking citizenship. It was supposed to make things easier. In too many cases, it didn't. I detailed some of the problems in a memorandum to DHS on November 24, 2003:

> Of the 130,000 U.S. soldiers deployed to Operation Iraqi Freedom, there are over 3,000 who are not US citizens. Judge advocates continue to help these soldiers file their initial naturalization applications. There is, however, no procedure for soldiers to complete interviews and undergo oaths in theater. There are over 70 soldiers who need to conduct these two steps. DHS has been requiring these soldiers to travel back to the United States to complete processing of their applications. As a result of our operational tempo and the inability of the command to lose soldiers weeks at a time, at least 55 soldiers have missed their interview appointments and at least 15 soldiers have missed their oath appointments since deployment to Iraq. Because of the inability to communicate effectively via telephone, email, or expedient mail with someone from the USCIS, many of these soldiers' files are now considered delinquent and their applications may be denied.

I pleaded with the DHS to send an agent to Iraq who could interview soldiers, process their citizenship applications, and conduct the oath ceremony, suggesting that they appoint a military contact at the USCIS to support soldiers during the process.

Nothing happened. Time after time, the USCIS refused to reschedule meetings in the United States for soldiers deployed in Iraq. Or they'd refuse to send the supplies we needed—like fingerprint sheets—to fill out our applications, expecting us to find them on our own in Iraq. Thanks but no thanks.

When I requested fingerprint sheets and ink pads from our military intelligence officers in the Green Zone, knowing they used them to process detainees, our request was ignored. One Friday, as we were pulling one of our convoys into the Green Zone, I told RV and Mac, "I don't know how, but by the time we leave here in two hours, I need you to have 120 fingerprint sheets and some ink pads." I'm still not sure how they got them.

It wasn't just wrong to delay citizenship to soldiers fighting for a country they couldn't even call their own; it was counterproductive. One paratrooper, Sergeant Sihoon Chung, who was born in South Korea and was nominated for a Bronze Star for his actions in Operation Iraqi Freedom, wanted to become a commissioned officer, but couldn't until he became a citizen. Another, Specialist Anis Attia, a native Tunisian and fluent Arabic speaker, wanted to become an intelligence analyst, but couldn't until becoming a citizen and earning a secret clearance. Talent was being kept from rising through the ranks as a result of bureaucratic foot-dragging.

But it was another case that always haunted me—that of Solomon Bangayan, a twenty-four-year-old Haitian immigrant from New York, assigned to the 82nd. An opportunity to help him came when New York senator Hillary Clinton visited that fall, leaving the safe confines of the airport to convoy to our FOB, one of only two senators to do so during my tour (the other was former 82nd paratrooper Jack Reed). When I saw Senator Clinton, I gave her a memo about Solomon, and her team back in Washington reached out to USCIS on his behalf. But on January 2, 2004, Solomon was riding in a convoy when an IED exploded underneath. It left a hole in the ground seven feet wide and three feet deep. Solomon died a hero. But he didn't want to be a hero—he wanted to be a U.S. citizen. Yet, despite our best efforts, his case was still being processed at the time of his death. In my mind, he was as much an American as anyone.

•

As angry as I was at the incompetence of the CPA, I was not surprised. The CPA's failure was emblematic of a larger failure. One of the key elements of good leadership is clear direction. But we never received any direction from the never-never land of the Green Zone. All we received were requests for reports. "Whatever you guys are doing," they would say, "let us know." They wanted just enough information to attend their briefings with Washington and appear as though they knew what was going on in the country they were supposed to be running.

None of this should have come as a surprise. In 2006, *Washington Post* writer Rajiv Chandrasekaran documented how key positions in the CPA were allocated on the basis of political ties rather than relevant experience. A twenty-four-year-old college graduate who had applied for a White House job was responsible for establishing Baghdad's stock exchange—even though he had never worked in finance. One of the people charged with managing Iraq's $13 billion budget had no background in accounting—but that didn't matter because she had a degree from an evangelical university. Chandrasekaran cited an e-mail from a former CPA employee describing the hiring process.

> I watched résumés of immensely talented individuals who had sought out CPA to help the country thrown in the trash because their adherence to "the President's vision for Iraq" (a frequently heard phrase at CPA) was "uncertain." I saw senior civil servants from agencies like Treasury, Energy . . . and Commerce denied advisory positions in Baghdad that were instead handed to prominent RNC [Republican National Committee] contributors.

As a result, the CPA was completely unequipped to serve as the governing authority in Iraq. One report to the Pentagon stated that despite having a staff of one thousand, the CPA had no mechanism to ensure that top-level decisions were executed at lower levels. It concluded, "There is a lack of internal unity of action." An army colonel I worked with and respect commented in Thomas E. Ricks's book *Fiasco* that his experiences at the CPA were like "pasting feathers together, hoping for a duck." The foundation of the entire American occupation had been built on quicksand. The weight was almost entirely on the military to somehow make a new democracy happen.

Allah's Will

By midsummer 2003, long before the schism in Islam became fashionable talk at Georgetown cocktail parties, the 2nd Brigade was confronting it in Al Rashid.

The differences between Sunni and Shia—something I knew little about before I got to Iraq—go back to the period immediately following the death of the Prophet Mohammed in 632 CE, when there was a dispute among the believers about who was the Prophet's rightful successor. Those who would come to be known as Sunnis argued that the elites in the community should pick a successor. Those who would come to be known as Shia (or Shiite) believed that the succession should stay within the Prophet's family by passing to Ali, who was married to Mohammed's daughter, Fatimah. This split has been used to justify war and persecution ever since.

There are about 1.3 billion Muslims in the world today. Shia make up somewhere between 10 and 15 percent of that total. But while they are the minority worldwide, they are the majority in Iraq, where they represent 60 percent of the population, which partly explains why Saddam Hussein, a Sunni, was so ruthless in persecuting them. For the most part, the Shia were not a constant threat in our district, although we were increasingly having trouble with the Dawa Party, a militant Shia group. Our primary threat emanated from the large Sunni community in our sector. Formerly the ruling elite, many Sunnis didn't trust the Western occupation and were deeply loyal to Saddam. The most extreme among them, Saudi Wahhabis, were particularly dangerous.

Every Friday, when mosques held regular services, several hateful sheikhs used their sermons to fuel sectarian strife in Al Rashid. These sermons often included calls to violence infused with anti-American, anti-Christian, and anti-Semitic propaganda. "We must kill the Americans and Jews who fight alongside them" was a frequent refrain. In our sector, we had 109 mosques. Our intelligence team monitored each one, usually sending a team or a friendly Iraqi nearby with a digital recorder to tape the sermons, which were often blasted on loudspeakers outside. Within months, we had determined that five mosques were pro-coalition, eighty-five were neutral, and nineteen were clearly anti-coalition. Not the sort of ratio we would have preferred.

•

One afternoon, as our second-battalion paratroopers were running a convoy in Al Rashid, they rounded a bend and saw a sight few live to recount: three Iraqis by the side of the road, one of them on his knees, with a rocket launcher on his shoulder aimed directly at their two vehicles, a two-and-a-half-ton truck and a

Humvee. There, right in front of them, a middle-aged Iraqi, in traditional Iraqi garb, was pulling the trigger again and again, but his rocket launcher was malfunctioning. Sensing that they were caught in a somewhat incriminating position, the Iraqis dropped their weapons, three AK-47s, their rocket launcher, and the components of an IED—and set off running.

Wasting no time, the paratroopers jumped out of their vehicles and chased down these insurgents. All those early-morning runs down Ardennes Street at Fort Bragg weren't for nothing. The leader of the three insurgents turned out to be a religious figure named Sheikh Tohma. Because he was a valuable detainee, Sheikh Tohma was transferred from a detainee cell at Baghdad International Airport to Abu Ghraib and finally to Camp Bucca, our top facility for enemy prisoners located near Umm Qasr in southern Iraq. After he was interrogated, Sheikh Tohma was put in a cell until we decided to bring him to trial.

The CPA's Ministry of Justice had recently established a court with a national jurisdiction, the Central Criminal Court (CCC), based in the Green Zone, intended to serve as Iraq's Supreme Court. The Iraqi government was looking for cases with a national dimension that could be brought before the CCC, and the leaders in the Green Zone had been asking us for months if we had any ideas.

Sheikh Tohma's case seemed a perfect fit. In a country increasingly torn by sectarian strife, trying him in a national court could help send the message that no one was above the law, not even religious leaders. The CPA's Ministry of Justice agreed. My brigade and battalion commanders even approved our request to pull two of the paratroopers who had been eyewitnesses off combat operations so they could testify—not an easy ask of infantry commanders who were already shorthanded.

Finally, in early January, several months after Sheikh Tohma had been apprehended, the case was ready for trial. I had our paratroopers prepped and ready to go. The night before, I called Camp Bucca and was assured that Sheikh Tohma would be on the convoy manifest to Baghdad the following day. I woke up at 4:45 a.m., went over my prepared case for what felt like the hundredth time, and called Camp Bucca again to confirm that Sheikh Tohma was on the manifest. After arguing with the soldier on the other end, who treated my call more as a nuisance than a security matter, I finally got my answer. "No, he's not on the manifest." After hurling a few expletives into the phone and quieting down, I was told that Camp Bucca had put Sheikh Tohma on the manifest for the wrong day.

Livid, I called the CCC, which was overseeing Sheikh Tohma's transportation, and explained the situation. They agreed to delay the trial for a day. I then had to notify the commanders of the soldiers who would be testifying. The next morning, I called Camp Bucca again to confirm that the sheikh was being transferred. Surely, in light of the previous day's error, they would take extra care this time. "We can't find him, sir." "What?!" I screamed into the phone. Apparently, as he was being prepped for transport to Baghdad, Sheikh Tohma had switched clothes, dug under a fence, and escaped. I wanted to go to Camp Bucca personally to ream someone out.

We soon realized there was one other—admittedly far less satisfying—option. I argued and convinced the CCC to try Sheikh Tohma in absentia for attempting to kill U.S. troops. I got the idea from the Philadelphia District Attorney's Office, which had done the same thing in 1993 against Ira Einhorn, a wealthy fugitive who had fled to France after being charged with the 1977 beating death of his girlfriend, Helen "Holly" Maddox.

Soon thereafter, the trial was back on. It was held just outside the Green Zone in the new courthouse in the Clock Tower Building, a short, sand-colored building with a steel tower sticking out the top. We weren't allowed to use our own translator, Alyaa, but I asked her to join me, anyway, to make sure nothing got by us. Meanwhile, despite some grumbling from the second battalion about our taking their men, I met with the two paratroopers. Neither of them had previously testified before an Iraqi judge, and they were nervous and suspicious. I had to convince them that the judge was our ally and that it was vital to describe as best they could the specific details of what had happened. When the judge asked one of them what his job was, the soldier replied, "I'm a 214 gunner," naming the large weapon he used as an infantryman. The judge was confused. He understandably didn't know what a 214 was, so I asked our paratrooper just to say that he served with coalition forces and was a member of the 82nd Airborne, kidding him afterward that he didn't have to be so specific about his weapon of choice that early in his testimony.

An hour into the trial, there was an explosion about a quarter mile away. A sergeant and I left the courtroom to see what had happened. It was a mortar attack. Undeterred, we continued with the trial. In the end, we got our conviction. It was a satisfying victory, but none of us had any illusions. We all felt certain that while he was being prosecuted in absentia, Sheikh Tohma was back on the streets, plotting another attack. And next time, he would use a weapon that worked. Despite the $2,500 bounty that Colonel Riley and General Dempsey put on his head, to the best of my knowledge, Sheikh Tohma has never been caught.

•

While mosques held their services on Fridays, St. Peter and St. Paul Catholic Church in Al Dora held Masses on Thursday nights. Built to help service the country's ancient Christian community, a community representing roughly 3 percent of the population at the time of the U.S. invasion, St. Peter and Paul's stood as a symbol of defiance in an increasingly militant Islamic neighborhood. By the time I left Baghdad, more than two hundred Christian Iraqis had been kidnapped, and at least sixty murdered. By 2007, 70 percent of Al Dora's Christians had been driven out.

Most weeks, a few of us from the 2nd Brigade would convoy on Thursday nights for 5:00 p.m. Catholic Mass—skipping every third or fourth week to avoid setting a pattern for insurgents. We'd take turns keeping watch outside so that everyone had a chance to pray, bringing our rifles inside with us, just in case, and placing them on the floor beneath our pews; we left our IBA vests and Kevlar helmets in the Humvees out of respect.

Hearing familiar hymns and taking the body of Christ in the Eucharist Communion always brought us comfort and solace in the midst of war. "Today at Mass," I wrote in my journal toward the end of my tour, "I stood next to an Iraqi worker, a man in his 40s. I helped him find the page in the song book then I pointed at what word/verse was being sung. I was filled with warmth as he tried to sing by keeping up. I felt as if my Lord, my God was talking through him."

Whenever we pulled up to St. Peter and St. Paul's, the church's orphans would come running. "Mister! Mister!" they would shout. *What did you bring us?* they'd ask with their eyes. I'd like to say the candy and small toys we brought were just for them, but they were for us, too—seeing those children smile gave us hope in our mission and in Iraq's future, just as similar smiles had given hope to Patty Ward during an earlier war. In their smiles the reality of our surroundings faded, and it was as if we were back someplace familiar, someplace where we belonged.

Thursday nights were also the customary time to hold weddings, and after Mass we'd often have to race toward gunshots, where guests had been firing weapons into the air to celebrate. Such celebratory fire was deadly. One of our brigade paratroopers, twenty-two-year-old specialist James Lambert, was smoking a cigarette inside our FOB when he was killed by a stray bullet from a nearby wedding on July 31—ten days before he was supposed to redeploy home.

One Thursday, after Mass, we raided three wedding ceremonies, kicking down doors and searching Iraqis' belongings for the weapons they had just fired. We were successful in only one of the raids. In the other two, we just found ammo and an AK-47, but it wasn't warm, evidence that it had not recently been fired. I rarely kicked down doors in Iraq, only a few times, but when I did, I tried my best to project strength and confidence to my team—even as my heart was in my throat the whole time, not knowing what awaited us on the other side.

Those Thursday nights were always filled with stark contrasts—children's smiles and needless deaths.

•

In 2003, Moqtada al-Sadr was not yet the notorious force in Iraq he would soon become, and his exact role in the ever-shifting Iraqi political landscape was far from clear. We now know he was honing his skills at the time, building a fleet of militant Shia followers called the Mahdi Army. But while we did not know all the details of al-Sadr's abilities and ambitions, even then we recognized him for what he was: a ruthless and incendiary figure with influence in every district in Baghdad.

One of Al Rashid's Shia leaders was an al-Sadr disciple, Sheikh Moyad. It was common practice in our district for Sheikh Moyad to justify acts of terror, theft, and vandalism by invoking Allah. Electric generators, cars, or weapons—he seized them all in the name of Allah. Even local Iraqis loathed him, blaming him for an attack on a liquor store that resulted in the death of a nine-year-old Iraqi girl. When questioned by Iraqi police, Moyad callously, but not surprisingly, attributed the girl's death to Allah's will.

We also had intelligence indicating that Moyad was not just using his Friday sermons to incite violence against our troops, but that he was using his mosque as a weapons depot—storing machine guns, mortars, and grenades there. But Moyad had been smart, carefully hiding his shadowy ties to militants. In addition, because of his influence and his stature as a religious leader, few Iraqis dared to challenge him. As a result, we had been unable to amass enough evidence to obtain an arrest warrant from our local Iraqi court, or even to get a judge with the courage to file charges.

But a few weeks into my tour, our brigade chaplain, Major John Murphy, was leading a convoy through Baghdad when an Iraqi came running toward him, arms flailing. Waving down the Humvee, the Iraqi—whom we would come to know as "Engineer Ali" on account of his profession—frantically described in broken English what had just happened to him.

Ali had been sitting with two friends outside his home when some of Sheikh Moyad's thugs came to seize their electric generator, which they had all chipped in to buy. In a city plagued by power failures, Sheikh Moyad believed he could hand out stolen generators for political favors or sell them at marked-up prices and keep the profits—in the name of Allah, of course. Ali and his friends protested. "You can tell that to Sheikh Moyad yourself," Moyad's henchmen forcefully countered, ordering them into the back of their car. Somehow, Engineer Ali had escaped.

When Ali finished his story, Chaplain Murphy, who at 6'1" stood several inches taller than Ali, said, "Do you know where your friends were taken?" Engineer Ali directed them to Sheikh Moyad's mosque. "Good, let's go get them. Mount up." Chaplain Murphy was always up for a mission, the more adventurous the better. A former infantry officer and jujitsu expert who shaved his head, he was no doubt one of the toughest chaplains on earth. Racing his convoy to the mosque, the chaplain and his men strode up to the entrance, guarded by men in black with AK-47s strapped behind their backs. Chaplain Murphy walked past them with his paratroopers and Ali trailing behind. Moments later, he was face-to-face with Sheikh Moyad. At first, the sheikh denied having anything to do with the theft of the generator. Then he claimed the generator had been seized in the name of Allah. That didn't cut it for Chaplain Murphy, who made it clear he was not leaving without Ali's companions. The sheikh freed them from a makeshift cell that had been built in the mosque; the generator was never returned.

Considering Moyad's stature in the community, I thought the CCC would also be interested in this case. Here we had direct evidence—in the form of a witness, Ali—linking Moyad to the kidnapping. That is, so long as Ali was willing to finger Moyad. Getting him to do that, it turned out, was not easy. "They'll kill me," he said. "They can't kill you if they can't find you," I replied. In the fall of 2003, the CPA didn't have anything like a witness protection program. But that kind of program was the only way we were going to get Ali to testify, so we had to create it. After weeks of prodding, the CPA agreed, thanks largely to my friend Judge Larry Rubini, a U.S. Army Reserve colonel from Bucks County, Pennsylvania, who was now at the CPA in a civilian capacity and who greased the skids to make this happen.

Finally, Ali agreed to testify, a courageous decision considering the risks. But Ali's father and two friends refused, imploring Ali to change his mind. "Think about your own safety," they urged him. "Think about your family." But Ali stood firm and gave us an affidavit identifying Moyad as the one responsible for the kidnapping and theft. I had it translated into English and sent to the CPA Ministry of Justice for processing in both English and Arabic. Surely such a sensitive document would be secure in their hands. Surely each of the few people who knew Ali's identity would want to protect him. Wrong. When word hit the streets that Ali was fingering Sheikh Moyad, Ali began receiving death threats. One day, it was a bullet on his car—a sign of an impending attack. Another day, strangers arrived at his home and left only after his wife lied and said Ali had just run out on her and their child and no longer lived there.

We had to bring this case to a successful completion as quickly as possible. We pulled an all-nighter drawing up charges based on the 1969 Iraqi Criminal Code, and got our arrest warrant from the CCC. Then there was another hitch. The Iraqi Police, citing the fact that Moyad was a religious leader, refused to arrest him. So Colonel Fuller ordered Operation Girth Hitch and sent Iraqi Police Special Forces, not the untrustworthy and corrupt regular police, to arrest Sheikh Moyad at his mosque. Moyad's followers, hoping to get some good press by portraying their sheikh as the

July 1964: Seaman
Apprentice Jack Murphy.
Courtesy of Marge Murphy

1965: My mother at the Immaculate Heart of Mary convent with her twin brother, Bill Rapone, before his deployment to Vietnam.
Courtesy of Marge Murphy

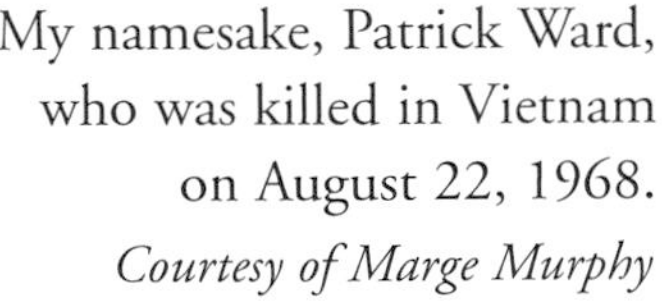

My namesake, Patrick Ward,
who was killed in Vietnam
on August 22, 1968.
Courtesy of Marge Murphy

Fall 1984: With my parents, en route to the sacrament of confirmation at St. Anselm's. *Courtesy of Marge Murphy*

February 16, 1996: Following the flood in Wilkes-Barre, I introduced President Bill Clinton when he visited King's College. *Courtesy of the author*

Spring 2002: Teaching the next generation of military officers at West Point.
Courtsey of Kitch Loftus-Mussari and Tony Mussari

Captain Patrick Murphy in Class-A uniform with the 82nd Airborne patch.
Courtesy of the author

October 2003: Taking five minutes to eat an MRE after a five-hour night mission.
Courtesy of the author

January 2004: In Baghdad, helping an Iraqi woman who filed a negligence claim against the U.S.
Courtesy of the author

In fall 2003 in Baghdad with my BOLT team and Alyaa. We gave those glasses to Iraqi orphans. *Courtesy of the author*

Fall 2003, Baghdad: Instructing the new "Airborne Iraqi" army soldiers on the rules of engagement.
Courtesy of the author

A rally with Senator John Kerry at my alma mater, Bucks County Community College; standing with us is Kevin Treiber, one of our hardworking veterans coordinators. *Ryan Neuls*

With Vietnam veteran and fellow army soldier, former senator Max Cleland. He and I share a moment of silent reflection at my VFW post in Croydon, Pennsylvania, in June 2006. *Ryan Neuls*

As we so often did during the campaign, the Murphy Corps volunteered in our community — here we help build a house in Langhorne, Pennsylvania, in January 2006. *Michael Fairchild*

Giving Alex Pitts a high five across the lawn from future Speaker of the House Nancy Pelosi after she spoke powerfully about the importance of stem cell research in August 2006. *Ryan Neuls*

In the closing days of the campaign, we held a standing-room-only house party with Senator Barack Obama. *Michael Fairchild*

My campaign staff with President Bill Clinton in Bristol, Pennsylvania, just days before the election — this was one of the high points of our campaign and we drew a crowd of more than four thousand. *Ryan Neuls*

With my Republican mother, Marge, as we go door-to-door to meet voters in Bristol in May 2006.
Ryan Neuls

With my friends in labor at the Philadelphia Labor Day parade in September 2006.
Ryan Neuls

Sitting next to Jenni with my shoes worn through, following what the *Philadelphia Inquirer* referred to as Murphy's "pounding of pavement" in the Eighth District.
Ryan Neuls

Jenni and I welcoming Margaret Grace — Maggie — to the world at Lower Bucks Hospital on November 24, 2006. *Courtesy of the author*

Swearing an oath to support and defend the U.S. Constitution with Speaker Nancy Pelosi and the Murphy family. *Courtesy of the author*

victim of Western aggression, claimed he had been arrested by coalition forces, but it was Iraqi Police Special Forces and we had the pictures to prove it. After the arrest, Iraqi Police Special Forces and paratroopers did a full sweep of Moyad's mosque as respectfully as we could. Just as our intelligence had reported, it was being used as a warehouse for AK-47s, grenades, and munitions.

The night of Moyad's arrest, a thousand Iraqis protested in the streets outside his mosque on one of the main roads in Baghdad, waiving Iraqi flags and chanting loudly. The protesters seemed to come from everywhere except our own district, where Moyad's crimes were well known. Busloads came from Sadr City by order of Moqtada al-Sadr himself. This wasn't one of those fake protests we heard were being ginned up with money from the Al Jazeera television network to give producers a good visual; this was the real thing.

Coordinating with General Dempsey of the 1st Armored Division, we lined up tanks to block Highway 8, and companies of paratroopers formed rows to push back protesters. Colonel Fuller also ordered support from military police, outfitted in riot gear. They stood in front of the paratroopers. A training grenade was tossed at our soldiers, injuring several military policemen; had it been a regular grenade, the result would have been catastrophic. But amid the chaos and scattered violence, not one round was fired by a paratrooper—a remarkable display of discipline and restraint. When a Red Crescent ambulance taking an injured Iraqi to the hospital was blocked by the crowd, we asked and then pleaded with the protesters to let the ambulance through, explaining that it was carrying one of their fellow countrymen. Predictably, they shouted back, parroting their leader, "If he dies, it will be Allah's will."

In several public appeals, I went on Iraq's national television, the Iraqi News Network (INN), and spoke through the network's female translator about the importance of establishing a rule of law, enumerating the charges against Moyad and presenting our evidence. Lies and exaggerations were all too common in Baghdad. In this case, false reports about why he was being arrested could further inflame the public. Afterward, Alyaa told me she had gotten a good laugh out of hearing me on TV with a woman's voice.

On top of all the legal footwork that went into the trial, there were additional precautions that had to be taken, like screening Iraqi judges so we could weed out those with Baathist ties.

Ultimately, we won a conviction, an important victory that made us proud. Sheikh Moyad was sentenced to six years in jail. But as long as Sheikh Moyad's master, Moquata al-Sadr, was out on the streets, we knew we'd be fighting the same battles again and again. If we truly wanted to restore a measure of law and order to Al Rashid—and Baghdad—we had to deal with al-Sadr himself. In August, we had our chance. As our case against Moyad was unfolding, a courageous Iraqi judge, Raid Juhi, issued a secret warrant for al-Sadr's arrest, implicating al-Sadr in the murder of Abdul Majid al-Khoei, a pro-coalition Iraqi exile and Shia rival, who was allegedly cooperating with the CIA.

Our brigade was selected to execute the arrest and began tactical planning, and I sat in on the meetings. We had intelligence on the routes he was taking. We had intelligence on his defenses—1,500 Mahdi Army soldiers in his mosque, and another 1,500 on standby at a nearby mosque. We were ready to move at a moment's notice. But we never got the green light we expected from the Green Zone, or from Washington.

I later learned what had happened. The operation was in its final stages, CPA official Dan Senor told *Newsweek* in 2006.

"We were down to figuring out the mechanisms of ensuring that the operation was seen as Iraqi, executed on an Iraqi arrest warrant," he said. "I remember it was late afternoon and we had just received . . . nine different questions [from Rumsfeld], rehashing how we were going to do this, to make sure it was not seen as an American operation."

Suddenly, the CPA got word that a powerful truck bomb had destroyed the Baghdad headquarters of the United Nations, an attack that left seventeen people dead, including the secretary-general's special representative for Iraq, Sergio Vieira de Mello. The bombing, according to Senor, was "a huge distraction, and the Sadr operation was forgotten."

The Bush administration's failure to seize al-Sadr was another missed opportunity—like losing bin Laden in the caves of Tora Bora in 2002, or failing to go after a senior al Qaeda leadership meeting on the border of Pakistan in 2005. Within months, the political landscape transformed, the rivalry between Shias and Sunnis exploded, and an attempt to seize al-Sadr became impossible without unacceptable political costs. For all their bluff and bluster, when decisive action was necessary, President Bush and Donald Rumsfeld didn't have the judgment to make the right call.

Democracy 101

Throughout my tour, there were occasional victories. One of them came in late July, when we got word that Saddam's sons, Uday and Qusay Hussein, had been killed. These guys were monsters. There were stories circulating about how Uday would rape the girlfriends of other prominent Iraqis and brand them with the letter U. It was also well known that he would torture members of the Iraqi Olympic team. One player who failed to measure up was dragged across a gravel pit, then dipped in a sewer so his wounds could fester. Uday's younger brother, Qusay, was also wicked. We were told he would watch as political prisoners were fed feetfirst into a wood chopper—if he were in a particularly brutal mood, he'd tell his henchmen to do it headfirst.

The night their deaths were announced, I gloated in my journal:

> 22 July Uday and Qusay killed. Hell yeah! Soon as it came out on Fox and Al Jazeera . . . celebratory fire erupted in Baghdad. We took positions on the roof to ensure force protection.

I added another line in my journal that night: "On a grimmer note, fedayeen drugging girls so they go place IEDs." Much of what was happening was "on a grimmer note." In the beginning, Iraqi children had run up to our tanks, waving at us and smiling. In a letter home to a grade-school class, I wrote, "The Iraqis here really love us. It is as if we are professional athletes, when we drive down the street the little kids (like 1st and 2nd graders) run out and wave at us." That still happened from time to time. But now, there were other stories—stories like the one about a soldier who went to slap the hands of a bunch of Iraqi children only to have one of the children slap a syringe needle into his palm. On one of our convoys, it wasn't waves that I saw, but an Iraqi boy giving us the finger. The only children we could always trust were the orphans at St. Peter and St. Paul's.

It didn't have to be this way.

•

I thought it was possible to establish a democracy in Iraq. But I also knew it was something that the Iraqis had to embrace and not something that could be imposed upon them. Building a democracy is never easy, especially in a country like Iraq with little sense of community and shared sacrifice. I tried to remain optimistic, remembering how our own nation had fought a bloody Revolutionary War, an even bloodier Civil War, and had been laboring for generations to live up to our founding ideals. I reminded myself that democracies have taken root in over eighty countries—including predominantly Muslim nations like Turkey and Pakistan—many of which did not have strong democratic traditions. These democracies aren't perfect, but democracy is never perfect. Still, they are examples of how it can work in different settings.

It didn't help when CPA administrator Paul Bremer decided to drive thirty thousand to fifty thousand members of Saddam's Baathist Party out of the government, including many experienced technocrats. But I didn't have much time to be concerned with establishing democracy in Iraq—my goal was establishing democracy in Al Rashid. Because our district was home to a quarter of Baghdad's population, it had its own District Advisory Council (DAC), an appointed group of Sunnis and Shia who met regularly and served as a branch of local government—setting up a health clinic, refurbishing schools, and making sure the water-treatment plant was working properly. During one meeting, when we were discussing the salaries council members would earn, a few of them started the usual complaints that they weren't being paid enough. "Why are we complaining about salaries?" one of them said to a colleague. "What we're doing is for our people, not for money. And besides, under Saddam, we didn't even get a bicycle for what we did." Unfortunately, this display of selflessness was uncommon.

We refurbished the council's meeting place with CERP money and held sessions we called Democracy 101. Things that we take for granted had to be taught from scratch. The councilmen had no idea, for example, how to set an agenda for a meeting. So we taught them a variation on Robert's Rules of Order. We also worked on similar issues with smaller Neighborhood Advisory Councils, and with bigger ones like the Baghdad City

Council and the Iraqi Governing Council, where as many as twenty-five members sat on each council.

But no matter how hard we tried—no matter how much the Iraqis on our council wanted to bring about democracy—there was always an invisible enemy working against us: fear. The fear of being killed kept many Iraqis from taking part in rebuilding their communities. They were terrified of working with American forces, lest they be deemed traitors. It was understandable. In September, Dr. Akila al-Hashimi, a member of the national Iraqi Governing Council, was assassinated outside her home in Al Rashid. From 2003 to 2007, several civilian leaders, thirty-one Iraqi judges, and a number of interpreters were killed. Fear is a part of everyday life in Baghdad, especially for those working with coalition forces.

•

Fresh out of Baghdad University, Alyaa was the first person in Al Dora, her religiously mixed neighborhood, to volunteer for American forces. She was eventually hired, and a while later her cousin Shaimaa started working as a translator as well. During my tour in Iraq, Alyaa was not just our BOLT teams interpreter, she was our guardian angel. Every day, our lives were in her hands. Whenever one of us met with an Iraqi who came to Scania to file a claim about damaged property or an injured loved one, she was by our side, helping translate the world around us. More than once she calmed down an Iraqi who had come to our FOB to threaten us or do us harm. She also protected us from Iraqis who were corrupt and had ulterior motives.

She traveled with us across Baghdad—from Scania to the CPA, from one courthouse to another—an indispensable part of our team. On one of those trips, we had to convoy past a traffic circle on the north side of the July 14th Bridge—named after the day in 1958 when Arab nationalists overthrew the monarchy. Sitting in the front of our lead Humvee as we rounded the bend, I watched in the rearview mirror as Alyaa slid right out of our newly steel-plated Humvee door, screaming as she fell to the pavement in midday traffic. Luckily, the trail vehicle behind us stopped before it hit her, leaving Alyaa with only a few minor injuries, which were patched up at our field hospital. She handled it with her usual good humor and, more than anything, was just embarrassed that she had ripped her blue jeans.

It was not easy for her to come to work each day under the hard stares of her neighbors. We slept in a fortified base, but not Alyaa. She returned each night to a neighborhood that was increasingly a hotbed for militants. She could have betrayed us. Other translators were allegedly text-messaging insurgents with information about troop movements. Militants offered good money for killing American soldiers, and Alyaa knew our whereabouts nearly every hour of every day. She could probably have supported her family for months on the money she would have received from turning on us. She could have made her own life—and the lives of her loved ones—easier by helping plan an ambush on our convoy. At the very least, she could probably have gotten the insurgents off her back by quitting her job. But she never did. With the strength, character, and courage of the toughest paratrooper in the 82nd, she always stood by us.

In return, we tried to look out for Alyaa. Because her neighbors knew where she and her cousin Shaimaa worked, we took extra convoys by their home to let those who might threaten them know they had our protection. But we were careful; we varied the time of day we went and the route we took, so watchful insurgents wouldn't be able to detect a pattern.

When it came time to leave Iraq, we all gathered in our FOB, and I read a few verses I'd hurriedly written, titled "A Poem to Princess Alyaa":

You are the legal princess
And now we must all confess
That we love you like our own sis
And more than anyone, you're the one we'll miss.

It certainly wasn't Shakespeare, but I hoped it gave her a sense of what she meant to us. Alyaa was tough as nails, but that day she cried. As a parting gift, she gave me a medallion to wear around my neck, next to with my crucifix and dog tags, containing three verses from the Koran. I wear it to this day.

A few months after I left Iraq, six sealed envelopes arrived at Alyaa's home—one for each family member who was working with American forces. They were signed by a group called the Jihad Units.

"You help the people you're supposed to fight," they read. "You deserve death."

The letter contained not just a threat, but a brutal warning: You have three days to post a notice at the local mosque that you are no longer working with the Americans, or you will be beheaded.

Alyaa and Shaimaa were terrified. But the insurgents didn't even give them a chance to comply. Before the deadline expired, they ambushed Shaimaa's father on his way to work. They shot him through the chest because he had dared to accept a job as a construction contractor for the CPA.

After the shooting, Alyaa and Shaimaa parted ways for their own safety. To stay ahead of the insurgents, Alyaa slept in a different friend's home whenever she could. But Shaimaa stayed behind and was there when the insurgents came back for her and her sister. Shaimaa was held in a single-room mud house outside Ramadi that doubled as a weapons stash. While she was there, her fiancé was murdered by the same men who had kidnapped her.

More than forty days later, Shaimaa was released—but only after her family had been driven into financial ruin to pay the exorbitant ransom the insurgents demanded. As Alyaa told Gaiutra Bahadur, the reporter who powerfully documented this story in the *Philadelphia Inquirer,* Shaimaa was "almost crazy" when she first got out. She didn't speak to anyone for a week. For months, she woke up in the middle of the night, shaking. She stayed away from her brother and didn't turn on the TV—her captors had warned her against it, saying it violated Islamic law. When she returned to her family, Shaimaa's forearms were bruised and her fingernails had slits in them from where her torturers attached cables to administer electric shocks.

Alyaa and Shaimaa's story is not unique. It is a story shared by many other ordinary Iraqis who risked their lives to work with coalition forces. There were many reasons Iraqis chose to work with us, some circumstantial, some financial. But at heart, every Iraqi I knew who signed up did so because he or she had a hunger for freedom and democracy that few who've never lived in a society ruled by tyranny or wracked by lawlessness can fully understand. It was their commitment to a brighter future for Iraq—their defiance of the fear that drove so many away from us—that renewed my hope in the darkest moments. And it is their strength and courage that will determine the success or failure of Iraq's democracy in the years ahead. It is with people like Alyaa and Shaimaa that Iraq's future now rests.

•

The worst mistake during a war that has become known for criminally negligent mistakes was the decision to disband the Iraqi Army. I was not alone in wondering why Paul Bremer made that decision. The Joint Chiefs of Staff were allegedly not consulted. Senior military officers thought it was a mistake. Secretary of Defense Rumsfeld and Secretary of State Powell were caught off guard. Although Bremer denied that he made this decision alone, as a result of it, hundreds of thousands of Iraqi soldiers were fired, creating overnight hundreds of thousands of unemployed, disgruntled, and armed Iraqi civilians. These soldiers could have helped us fight the insurgency. Instead, many of them became part of it.

Despite the reputation of the Iraqi Police (IP) for corruption, we initially tried to work with them to bring about law and order. We raised the IP pay by several dollars a month and laid out a standard of no tolerance toward corruption. Success was fleeting. Within a few months, we fired sixty police officers, but the corruption persisted.

As a result, the decision was made to establish another force, what we called the Iraqi Civil Defense Corps (ICDC), now called the Iraqi Army. At first those in Washington considered calling it the New Iraqi Army (NIC), until they realized that *Nic* is an obscenity in Arabic. The ICDC was intended to serve as a paramilitary force—in a sense, an Iraqi National Guard. The task of recruitment fell to a number of units, including ours. We posted flyers all over Al Rashid. Despite recruiting in a district where U.S. soldiers had good reason not to take too many convoys outside the wire and Iraqis had good reason to stay home, we were successful and especially proud when 360 Iraqis showed up one Saturday to join.

As part of the ICDC, Iraqis were sent away for a weeklong training that was run by the U.S. military. But when they came back, it was clear they hadn't learned even the basics. Many didn't know how to handle their weapons properly. One Iraqi soldier purposely fired his weapon into the air when a civilian started cursing at him. On operations with U.S. soldiers, the Iraqis wouldn't take orders, or they'd flee when the fighting started. They didn't even have uniforms and we had to give them Chicago White Sox caps so they had some way of identifying themselves.

It was an unacceptable situation; without metrics that told us where they were falling short in training, we were discovering their shortcomings during patrols when lives were at stake. We could hardly blame the Iraqis: Most of us initially had six to eight weeks of basic training and then months of highly sophisticated advanced training. They were given a week to become professional soldiers. But there was no time for excuses or finger pointing; we had to get them up to speed.

The 82nd took the initiative. Our brigade began our own additional weeklong training for ICDC soldiers. Our BOLT team convoyed to the base just south of our FOB and held classes there, training somewhere between fifty and a hundred Iraqis a week. Other members of the brigade trained them in first aid, military marksmanship, and operations. Our team's portion took up more than two hours and focused on the laws of war. No one told us what to say. But with Alyaa translating our handouts into Arabic, and RV, Santi, Three-Shot, Mac, Sergeant Robinson, and me lecturing on the rules of engagement, we were a strong team.

There were around sixty people in each class. I'd start off by saying that in America, the military is the most respected profession, as it is in many countries around the world. The reason is that soldiers abide by seven army values: loyalty, duty, respect, selfless service, honor, integrity, and personal courage. The first value was summed up by a quote in the police movie *Striking Distance*—"Loyalty above all except honor." There was loyalty to the guy by your side, but more than that, there was loyalty to your country—which sometimes meant reporting those who were being disloyal. Then there was duty and respect. Selfless service meant putting your country ahead of your own needs. "So what if you're tired when your country needs you? You can sleep when you're dead," I said with a wry smile, the effect delayed until the translation hit their ears. Honor meant doing the right thing in the eyes of Allah. I told them what integrity meant by describing an Iraqi soldier who turned in a paratrooper who had stolen money from an Iraqi family during a raid. The paratrooper was court-martialed, and they would meet the same fate if they didn't serve honorably. I'd close with personal courage, saying that when bullets are flying, it's easy to let someone else do the fighting. There was always silence when I said this, and I looked into their eyes. Whether they are in Iraq or at West Point, students can tell when a teacher is speaking from the heart. They could sense that we were serious, and I could sense their unspoken commitment to the fight.

They were excited about the additional training—in part because we kept telling them this was special airborne training, and we gave them airborne wings to pin to their uniform when it was all over, even though they didn't jump out of any airplanes. All in all, we trained more than six hundred Iraqis from the fall to the winter. All of them but one were men. The one woman in the group joined with her teenage son, and while she may have received gentle ribbing from her classmates, we were all proud of her. In our last session together, I told them that twenty years from now, I hoped to take my future family to Iraq on vacation to show them what an extraordinary place it is—with its beautiful palaces and generous people. And I'd ask them to do their part to make that future possible.

We hoped the extra training was effective, but frankly, extra training shouldn't have been necessary. All along, we knew that for U.S. forces to leave, the Iraqis would have to be prepared to secure their own country. "As the Iraqis stand up, we will stand down"—that's what President Bush had said, over and over again. But once again, his rhetoric didn't match his record.

During a House Armed Services Committee hearing in my first few months as a congressman, I had the chance to put the training question directly to General Peter Pace, chairman of the Joint Chiefs. I asked if any thought had been given to training Iraqis either outside Iraq or in remote Iraq. "When I went to Fort Knox," I said, "I wasn't going to the Jersey Shore on a weekend. I was going to basic training because it's a profession. It's something that you have to take very seriously. You can't be worrying about your family back at home or your imam back at home. . . . So is there a thought on changing the way we train these soldiers so as to make sure . . . they understand how to take orders for one Iraq and not for a certain imam?" General Pace's reply: "I'll check on that."

When one of General Pace's top deputies called me back, I pressed him on how many basic-training sites existed in Iraq. The number was three. It came as little surprise when the White House said in May 2007 that training Iraqis was not one of our primary missions. What should have been a top priority was treated like busywork.

•

From the start, reconstruction efforts were plagued by corruption. To date, the United States has spent more than $30 billion on reconstruction in Iraq, at least $8.8 billion of which has vanished according to our Government Accountability Office, no doubt filling the coffers not just of greedy Iraqi politicians but of warlords and insurgents. It was infuriating to hear reports of crates full of U.S. currency going missing and to witness other forms of corruption firsthand.

When it became clear that a member of the Baghdad City Council, a charismatic politician named Majed, was diverting coalition money into his own pocket, our BOLT team drafted the charges that led to his arrest. We were disappointed in Councilman Majed, who shared responsibility for the 5.5 million Iraqis living in Baghdad. Paratroopers and Iraqis alike had come to appreciate and respect his efforts, and he was widely viewed as someone who could have been a great leader in Iraq. But we had to set an example. We had a zero-tolerance policy toward corruption.

There are few better examples of how corruption has undermined security and stability than Iraq's black market in oil. Iraq has the world's second-largest known oil reserves—which is why one of the war's architects, Deputy Defense Secretary Paul Wolfowitz, actually claimed the war would pay for itself. But vast amounts of Iraq's oil profits were being pocketed by corrupt vendors rather going toward reconstruction projects for the Iraqi people. As a result of these and a variety of other problems—including attacks by insurgents on oil pipelines and an inability to refine oil—there were artificial oil shortages throughout the country. Iraqis spent hours waiting in lines miles long to buy gas for their cars and liquefied petroleum gas (LPG) to heat their homes.

One day, as we were observing Iraqis handing out LPG, the people in line at the gas station started asking for two liters instead of the usual one. In a kindhearted gesture, they were given two liters if they had just lost a family member and brought the death certificate as proof. But the next day, every Iraqi seemed to have a death certificate, even if it was months old or clearly altered.

Growing violence was another result of these large crowds. We were convoying back to our FOB one day when we saw a disturbance at a nearby gas station. As we got closer, Iraqis rushed up to our Humvee, screaming in Arabic. "What are they saying?" I asked. Alyaa, in her usual seat directly behind me, shouted in my ear, "There's a man who just shot at the people and the Iraqi police. He's in a black BMW, he's a bad man, they're asking us to get him." As if on cue, we saw the black BMW speed off fifty feet away. The Iraqi police did not have vehicles to give chase, but we did. RV was driving our Humvee and Santi was the gunner. "Let's get 'em, RV. Don't let him get away." I radioed to our trail vehicle, letting them know that we were responding to this disturbance, and called it in to our FOB, in case there were other paratroopers in the vicinity who could help.

As we chased the BMW, RV was literally standing on the pedal. But we couldn't keep up, and Santi wisely didn't fire his mounted SAW machine gun from the turret above, since there were too many civilian vehicles and personnel on the streets.

Shortly afterward, General Dempsey ordered a mission called Iron Justice I, which resulted in the capture of twenty-eight fuel trucks and nine propane trucks that were illegally dispensing fuel. It was followed by Iron Justice II, a similar crackdown on black-market sales. We did not target individual street-side vendors, instead focusing on the twelve fuel stations in Al Rashid, each seemingly charging whatever price they wanted for government oil. To the gas station owners, our message was clear: If they didn't comply with Iraqi law, they would be fired by the Ministry of Justice and forbidden to sell gasoline. Considering how big the problem was, we wouldn't be able to solve it alone. But we had to do something. Coalition forces were usually the only honest broker in Iraq—not because Americans are more honest than Iraqis, but because in most cases, we had what we needed and couldn't be paid off or intimidated with violence.

•

We were never going to bring about peace and stability, not like this. The words of General Shinseki and General Powell rang in my ears. They were right: Stability required overwhelming force.

But America's military experts were marginalized by civilians in the Bush administration if they did not toe the line. General Shinseki, a West Point graduate and decorated Vietnam War veteran, was shunned as army chief of staff, and his rift with the civilian leadership reached breaking point when he testified to the Senate Armed Services Committee on February 25, 2003, a few weeks before the invasion of Iraq:

> Something on the order of several hundred thousand soldiers are probably, you know, a figure that would be required. We're talking about post-hostilities control over a piece of geography that's fairly significant, with the kinds of ethnic tensions that could lead to other problems. And so it takes a significant ground-force presence

> to maintain a safe and secure environment, to ensure that people are fed, that water is distributed, all the normal responsibilities that go along with administering a situation like this.

Immediately and publicly, Defense Secretary Don Rumsfeld called Shinseki's estimate "far off the mark." Two days after Shinseki testified, Secretary Wolfowitz appeared before the House of Representatives:

> There has been a good deal of comment—some of it quite outlandish—about what our postwar requirements might be in Iraq. Some of the higher-end predictions we have been hearing recently, such as the notion that it will take several hundred thousand U.S. troops to provide stability in post-Saddam Iraq, are wildly off the mark. It is hard to conceive that it would take more forces to provide stability in post-Saddam Iraq than it would take to conduct the war itself and to secure the surrender of Saddam's security forces and his army—hard to imagine.

When General Shinseki retired after thirty-eight years of service, his civilian leaders Rumsfeld and Wolfowitz did not even attend his farewell ceremony. They could have learned something if they had. At the ceremony, General Shinseki delivered a remark that would prove prophetic:

> Beware the 12-division strategy for a 10-division Army. Our soldiers and families bear the risk and the hardship of carrying a mission load that exceeds what force capabilities we can sustain, so we must alleviate risk and hardship by our willingness to resource the mission requirements.

By fall we had 148,000 troops on the ground in Iraq for 25 million Iraqis. We knew it wouldn't be enough, especially since there were so few State Department personnel around. In Al Rashid, we had 3,500 soldiers to secure 1.5 million Iraqis—one for roughly every 400 Iraqis. According to our counterinsurgency doctrine, it should have been one for every 50 Iraqis, a minimum force of 30,000. Even in my hometown, Philadelphia, which had the same-size civilian population as Al Rashid, my father was one of 7,000 cops patrolling the streets. Here, we didn't speak the same language; and the population was armed, often with AK-47s or more powerful weapons, and we had roughly half as many cops as Philly. Using our counterinsurgency formula in Iraq as a whole, we should have had about 500,000 troops on the ground, not 148,000.

In Bosnia, no American lives were lost, $6 billion was spent, and we followed the military doctrine of one soldier for every fifty civilians because the Clinton White House heeded the counsel of the Pentagon's military experts. As I write this, there have been more than 3,900 American deaths and $600 billion spent in Iraq, and not enough troops because the Bush White House refused to listen to our leadership at the Pentagon.

A foreign occupation is like a broken bone—it has to be set properly from the beginning, otherwise tendons and muscles will grow around the break, making it difficult, if not impossible, to correct. Without sending enough troops to get the job done, America's efforts were doomed from the start.

•

Maybe it would have been different if more generals had possessed the courage to speak truth to power. There is a long tradition in the military of generals standing up to their civilian leaders. During World War II, General Dwight Eisenhower, as Supreme Allied Commander, wasn't initially given the unity of command over American and British air forces he believed he needed to lead and support his Allied ground troops in Operation Overlord. He literally threatened to resign. But President Roosevelt listened to his number one military expert, Eisenhower, and agreed to give him what he needed. Eisenhower set the standard of how a general should act.

Many Vietnam-era generals set the standard of how not to act. Every officer in the United States Army is expected to conduct professional reading and on top of every list is former West Point professor Colonel H. R. McMaster's 1997 insightful book, *Dereliction of Duty*. Colonel McMaster's premise is that during Vietnam instead of fulfilling their duty to resign or stand by the courage of their convictions, "five silent men" at the top of our military did nothing, allowing themselves to be marginalized, and allowing troops to be sent to Vietnam without a true strategy. This "dereliction of duty" led to a mismanaged war and contributed to the deaths of fifty-eight thousand brave American troops. Army Chief of Staff General Harold K. Johnson always regretted his failure to resign in protest during the Vietnam War. "I am now going to my grave with that lapse in moral courage on my back," he remarked.

It may take years—even decades—to fully uncover and understand what happened behind closed doors in the Bush White House and Pentagon during 2002 and 2003. But prior to our invasion, our military leaders were aware that tactics such as roadside bombs could be used. Prior to our invasion, it was clear that we would need far more troops in Iraq to get the job done. Our generals had a moral obligation to tell their civilian leaders what they needed to hear, not what they wanted to hear, about the costs of invasion. Too many did not.

In 2007, seven deployed active-duty army soldiers from the 82nd Airborne Division spoke out, writing an op-ed piece in the *New York Times* titled "The War as We Saw It," questioning the so-called progress that was being made in Iraq. "To believe that Americans, with an occupying force that long ago outlived its reluctant welcome, can win over a recalcitrant local population and win this counterinsurgency is far-fetched," they wrote. "We need not talk about our morale. As committed soldiers, we will see this mission through." It was a display of candor and courage that their superior officers could have taken a lesson from. The article appeared in late August. In early September, two of the authors, Sergeant Omar Mora and Sergeant Yance T. Gray, were killed in a vehicle accident in western Baghdad. Another, Staff Sergeant Jeremy A. Murphy, was shot in the head as the article was being written.

And yet the sad truth is that even if all our generals had spoken out with the courage General Eisenhower displayed during World War II, or General Shinseki displayed in 2003, or these seven active-duty soldiers displayed in 2007, this White House would likely not have listened to them.

The Heartache of Homecoming

"Thank God it's December," I wrote in my journal on December 1, 2003. "November was the deadliest month in the war." It only got worse. On Christmas Eve, at a candlelit service at our new consolidated FOB, near our previous FOB at Scania, we all sang "Silent Night" to the whistles of 105-millimeter mortars falling in the distance. It turned out to be the largest offensive by insurgents since my arrival.

A few weeks earlier, right before Sunday services, our operations major came up to me and said, "Murph, we found number one." Saddam Hussein was caught cowering in a six-foot-deep "spider hole" in Tikrit. We were all glad to hear it, but we also knew it was largely symbolic. There was no gloating in my journal that night, no "hell yeah!" as there had been when Uday and Qusay were caught.

This time, there was just a question: "What will happen now?"

•

As my tour came to a close, I began training my replacement, an officer I knew slightly from my deployment to Bosnia. One day, discussing the challenges his team would face, he made a confession. "After you leave, Murph, we're not leaving the wire. It's too dangerous. We're just not trained for it." My heart sank. I couldn't believe it. "You think we were trained for this?"

All that we had accomplished—from carrying out small acts of justice to prosecuting bad imams—had been possible because we were willing to leave our FOB, get out into the city, talk to Iraqis, and rattle the bureaucracy of the Green Zone. It was impossible for me to imagine doing our job any other way. How can you help a country if you're afraid to set foot in it? A call to Colonel Riley did nothing—my job would now be done by another, who had his own way of doing things. I had to accept it.

When we finally got our orders to redeploy, as close as I had grown to my friends over there, as much of myself as I felt I had given to the country, I was ready to leave. I was ready to drive down a street without worrying about scanning the curbs for IEDs, the rooftops for snipers, or looking back to see if the trail vehicles in my convoy were still behind me.

I left Iraq in late January, seven months after I got there. Most of the brigade senior staff left around the same time. On my way back, I had the company of RV and Santi. Mac had left a week earlier, Three-Shot Broussard a couple days ahead, and Sergeant Robinson four weeks earlier. The trip took us from Baghdad to Balad Air Base, roughly forty miles north, to an air force base in Spain, and from there to the United States.

While we were in Balad, RV turned to me and asked me one of his purposeful questions, this one about the country we were leaving. "Sir, what were we doing here? What really was our mission?" It was a question he'd asked me before but one I had brushed off. Now I attempted to give him an answer, one that was never articulated to me, but one that I had pieced together from my own experience.

"Our mission here," I told him, "is threefold: first, to capture Saddam Hussein, which we did up in Tikrit; two, to find those weapons of mass destruction, which looks at this point like they were never here; and lastly, to give the Iraqis some form of representative government, which we are trying to build." "Hopefully," I added, "we won't suffer from 'mission creep,'" which happens when a war's aims expand beyond what they were originally intended to be, as occurred in Vietnam.

My last night in-country was bittersweet. I had given everything I had and was physically and emotionally exhausted. But I was also incredibly proud of everyone I had served with—from the paratroopers in my BOLT to the eleven Bravos, the infantrymen paratroopers who kicked down most of the doors, did most of the fighting, and saw the true horror of war. But beyond any individual soldier, it was the teamwork within our brigade of 3,500 paratroopers that was most inspiring. And it worried me that we were leaving two other members of our team, Alyaa and Shaimaa, behind.

•

When we stepped off the C-130 at Pope Air Force Base in North Carolina, we were greeted by the 82nd Airborne band, my brigade commander and sergeant major, and a crowd waiving "Welcome Home Airborne" signs. Standing with the other families who had gathered to await their loved ones at the hangar were my parents, my sister and her husband, Brian, from

Colorado, my brother, J.J., and his wife, Colleen, from Wilkes-Barre, and all my nieces and nephews. Standing behind my family was Ashley, looking awkward. We all celebrated by going out to IHOP.

After lunch, driving to my apartment, Ashley said, "I can't do this anymore," as she looked straight ahead, continuing to drive. I was not surprised. It had been hard keeping our relationship together while I was in Iraq. After she left that July, I had been confident we could make it work. But as the months passed, there was no telling when I'd return. By the end of August, she was back in the United States, and soon after, her letters tapered off. In September, we spoke by phone. Her words of devotion remained, but her tone had changed dramatically. I sensed the flame was out. As I handed the satellite phone back over to Major Eubanks, the signal officer I deployed with, he saw my ashen face and asked, "What's up, Murph?" "I'm good, sir" I managed, as the lump in my throat started choking me. I was down, but I never told my men or my colleagues; I needed to be the one motivating them and couldn't show any emotional weakness. But my attempt to hide my heart didn't fool all those who knew me. At about 2:00 a.m. that night, hours after my call with Ashley, I went up onto the roof, where RV was at the security nest, manning the large .50-caliber machine gun. I handed him a soda and a Snack Pack. After a minute, he asked, "What's up, sir?" He could tell. "Nothing," I said. "It's all good. How's it going for you?" I was hurting, but dragging others down made no sense. I wasn't going to feel sorry for myself. As hard as it was, others saw long marriages fall apart, sometimes losing custody of their children. Many times, I was the one counseling these paratroopers, so I knew I had it easy.

But now, in the car, listening to her say those words, it hit me hard. I asked repeatedly if there was someone else, if we could work things out. I knew she had checked out emotionally months earlier, but had held out hope that, once I was home, the flame would reignite. I was wrong. She had moved on. I later found out that since our telephone conversation back in September she had been dating someone else—"Jody" is what soldiers call the other guy. I felt empty and confused. This wasn't supposed to happen when you came home from war. When I told my parents the next morning at the nearby Fayetteville hotel that our engagement was off, the tears finally—and uncontrollably—started coming.

The army marching cadence "When I Get On Back Home" played over and over again in my head, a cadence that now felt like it was taunting me ten years after I first sang it.

Used to date a beauty queen
Now I date my M16

Ain't no use in looking down
Ain't no discharge on the ground

Ain't no use in going back
Jody's got your Cadillac

Ain't no use in calling home
Jody's got your girl and gone

Said it won't be long,
Till I get on back home

A couple of weeks later, in February 2004, I was notified that I and some members of the brigade senior staff would be awarded the Bronze Star for service. My own medal narrative was a testament to what our brigade had accomplished up until November 2003.

> After months of combat operations, including over 15,191 patrols, 339 raids, 1838 detainees captured, 23 enemy wounded, and at least 137 enemy killed-in-action, there have been no founded reports of law of land warfare violations within the brigade combat team. . . . CPT Murphy was the Convoy Commander in over 75 movement-to-contact missions throughout the Baghdad area of operations, one receiving small arms fire, but all resulting in mission accomplishment and no soldiers killed or wounded in action. . . . [He] was the only trial counsel in Baghdad to successfully prosecute two Central Criminal Court cases in Iraq, one which was the first case against an imam and the other the first case against a Baghdad city councilman. . . . [He] led the premier Foreign Claims Commission in Iraq. As of 15 November 2003, over 1129 claims were adjudicated by the brigade under the Foreign Claims Act, a highly complicated process which has also proven to be an invaluable tool in winning the hearts and minds of the Iraqi people. Of these 1129 claims adjudicated, 198 of them were paid, totaling $120,080. In comparison, 4th ID adjudicated 148 claims, 3rd COSCOM adjudicated 15, and the other 11 brigades in 1st AD adjudicated 878.

There was a ceremony, but because my family was in Pennsylvania and couldn't make it, I asked Ashley to attend. I still hadn't had the heart to tell my army buddies that she had dumped me. I was trying to stay friends with her, and it was a big day for me—one I wanted to share. She said she'd be there, but she was a no-show.

I thought about Koby Langley after my engagement fell apart. We had stayed in touch after he left Iraq, and he told me that the hardest day of his life was the day he returned home. He left with a feeling that the mission was going to turn into a bloodbath, and that the Iraqis would never sacrifice more than they had to while we were there, that the mission was fundamentally flawed. When he got home he knew that he would be leaving the unit he loved and the people he served with to take what he frustratingly called "a desk job" in Washington, D.C. And he also knew that when he stepped off that plane, the one person who should have been there, the one person he wanted to be there, would not be there: his wife.

Koby never spoke openly to anyone about what happened, but he made it clear to me that at the end of the day, he felt he had failed in his marriage. Taking responsibility is just a part of who he was, who we all are as army officers, but I have my suspicions that as in the song, "Jody" got his girl, too.

•

Koby and I were not alone. What many soldiers have learned is that there are some people in your life who can accept the sacrifices that are needed to keep a military family together and others who cannot. With the unprecedented policies of endless and prolonged deployments in Iraq, many soldiers today—and their families—have been asked to give up too much. They have been asked not only to focus on a nearly impossible mission abroad, but to keep things together back home, while their deployments stretch from six, then to nine, then twelve, and even fifteen months. Troops are returning to Iraq in historically high numbers unseen in modern-day warfare. In World War II, 245 days of combat, or eight months, was the benchmark for when the GI suffered neuropsychological disease. One in four did, according to Ken Burns's documentary *The War*.

Today's current personnel policies are designed to keep soldiers from retiring or leaving at the expiration of their contractual obligation. The military is breaking its word, at the direction of "the decider," and the current state of personnel policies has been described by military leaders as "archaic" and "barbarous." As Pennsylvania senator Bob Casey said, "These fighting men and women were born into families, not into divisions and brigades."

Graduates of West Point are leaving active duty at the highest rate in decades. The divorce and separation rates in the military have reached historic highs as soldiers return to Iraq for their second, third, and fourth time. The military's suicide rate is at an all-time high for the last twenty-six years, with ninety-nine troops taking their life in 2006, and almost a thousand others attempting suicide—a tragic trend we witnessed firsthand when a paratrooper in our brigade took his own life while pulling security one night in Baghdad. Sadly, we were only weeks away from going home.

Instead of wondering if soldiers' families will be there when they return to help them heal from the physical or psychological ravages of war, the odds are now greater than ever that they should now expect that they won't be—another failure of the Bush administration's policy, and one that a simple resignation by Secretary Rumsfeld will never fully account for. The Bush administration's policies in Iraq not only have cost the lives of the servicemen and -women who readily gave them, they have ripped apart the moral fabric of our great military—the families of our servicemen and -women.

Our policies had to change. The war in Iraq had to come to an end. And I was about to discover that my fighting days were far from over.

PART III

TAKING THE HILL

Success doesn't go to the strongest or the smartest, but to the one who has the greatest will.

—Vince Lombardi

The Home Front

All veterans carry the burden of war in our hearts, and it affects us in different ways. While I tried to focus on the good I saw in Iraq, the evil of some Iraqis would revisit me in my dreams. I didn't sleep much those first weeks back. Many veterans of past wars told me that the hardest thing to do is to come home from war. They were right. The loss of nineteen of my fellow paratroopers weighed on my heart.

It helped to get away for a while, first with Chris Norbeck and some buddies for a five-day trip to Florida, and then to Colorado to visit my sister Cathy's sixth-grade social studies class. I told her class the G-rated version of my tour, such as what it was like to swim in Saddam's palace pools and how it got to 138 degrees in August, and how it took a while to adjust to the Iraqi custom of kissing men hello three times on the cheek. "I wasn't used to it," I said, and the kids giggled.

I was peppered with all sorts of questions, some routine, some probing, but each innocent. There were a few easy questions—like whether I knew my sister recently sent in a photo of me to appear on *The Bachelor* TV show (this caught me by surprise), and what my three rows of medals stood for. Others were more reflective. A sixth-grade boy named Julian asked: Were Iraqis different from Americans? "Not really," I replied. "Most Iraqis want what we do: peace, security, good-paying jobs so they can feed their family, and they like to play sports, too, like soccer, just like we do." Another, from a girl named Ana: What was the most valuable lesson you learned? "To treat people as you want to be treated. I'm also more grateful for the little things," I told them, "like falling asleep on the couch watching TV." A young boy named James excitedly asked the last question, which I should have been ready for but somehow hit me like a ton of bricks. "Did you see anyone get hurt?" My face turned white, and my mind raced—not only to the paratroopers who had been killed and wounded, but also to the Iraqis I had encountered who had been killed and wounded. After a pause, I swallowed and answered slowly, "Yes, James, I saw some people get hurt, and some people who even died. That is the unfortunate thing about war, and why I hope and pray we don't have any more of it." I looked into James's eyes as he sat there on the ground, and then scanned the rest of the eleven- and twelve-year-old faces. There was a silence, an understanding, and an education for each of us.

The vacation was much needed. It helped to be with family and friends, and relax a little. Unlike the elementary school students, my family thoughtfully didn't ask a lot of questions, which also helped me avoid dwelling on the past. I quickly found that the best way for me to readjust was to dive into work.

From February to September, I was one of the trial counsels at Fort Bragg, prosecuting soldiers who broke the law—in most cases, the Uniform Code of Military Justice. That year, I prosecuted thirteen courts-martial, earning a conviction in each. Most of the time, I was the lead prosecutor.

In one disturbing case, a supply sergeant from our 2nd Brigade Combat Team was accused of stealing a shipment of laptop computers when they arrived in Baghdad, and selling them for thousands of dollars in personal profit to a local Iraqi civilian. He was rightfully convicted. Another sad trial involved a paratrooper who had served honorably in Iraq, leading a squad of eight paratroopers, but went AWOL after his monthlong "block leave" vacation—a war hero who'd suddenly become a fugitive. When the military police officers went to his home in West Virginia and knocked on his front door, instructing him to let them in, he ran out the back—and into the waiting hands of law enforcement. While my job was to ensure justice was being served, it still pained me to prosecute my own.

When the story broke about abuse at Abu Ghraib, I was in Colonel Fuller's office at Fort Bragg, watching FOX News. "That just set us back in the Mideast by ten years," Colonel Fuller said. I fear his estimate was on the low end. The crimes of Abu Ghraib undermined both our efforts to build trust with Iraqis and our claims to moral leadership in the world. I was ashamed and embarrassed by these soldiers' lack of professionalism. And I was angry. Those crimes endangered our troops still serving. There is no doubt in my mind that American soldiers died because some Iraqi who otherwise would have stayed home decided to seek vengeance.

•

Eventually, while I knew in my heart I still wanted to serve my country, I realized that after two deployments, a failed wedding engagement, and the constant moving around, it was time to return home to Pennsylvania. I was proud of what I had achieved in the army—personally and professionally—but I didn't feel a calling to continue being a career soldier. It had been more than ten years since I first wore the uniform and I was looking for something new. At first, I thought I might return to the law, but reentering the Philadelphia legal profession from North Carolina proved difficult. My blue-collar background and years in the army didn't come with many connections. Firms in the Philadelphia area weren't exactly beating down my door; they weren't sure to what extent my nineteen- and twenty-hour days in Iraq would translate into billable hours. My old firm, Murphy & O'Connor, which had fewer than twenty-five attorneys, thought they might have a spot for me as an associate attorney, but even that possibility later fell through.

In hindsight, I'm glad it did. As the months passed, I had time to reflect on what I had seen in Iraq. At that point, I was still developing my thoughts on what needed to be done. But I knew the Bush administration's handling of the war had been criminally negligent. And I felt a responsibility to help bring about a change in our policy. I had supported President Bush in the aftermath of 9/11. But he had betrayed our nation's trust. It was time to volunteer for a different kind of public service.

•

The day I was discharged from Fort Bragg in September 2004, I drove all night to Philly and showed up to volunteer the next morning at the offices of the one person I felt could bring about the change we needed in the war: Vietnam veteran and Democratic presidential nominee Senator John Kerry. The idea of volunteering on the Kerry campaign had been suggested by Tom Leonard, a political genius who grew up with my mom and Patty Ward, and was active in Democratic politics in Pennsylvania.

I had been told to show up at 7:30 a.m.; when I arrived early, at 7:00 a.m., the doors were still locked and there was no one in sight. So I leaned against the wall and read the morning's paper, hoping someone would show up soon. When a staffer finally came to open the office twenty minutes later, I introduced myself and let him know it was my first day. I was a little surprised that he was dressed in ripped jeans and a T-shirt; I was wearing a suit. But even after I learned that most people dress casually on a campaign, I continued to dress formally—an old army habit, I guess. No wonder someone joked that I "looked Republican."

When I started volunteering, I had no idea what I would be doing. At some point, I was tasked to be a veterans' coordinator, along with fellow Iraq vet Jon Soltz, a young army captain who had also served in Baghdad in 2003. He handled the western half of Pennsylvania, working out of the campaign's Pittsburgh office. Together we ran a veterans outreach program, each of us speaking on behalf of Senator Kerry at colleges, American Legion and VFW halls, and rallies across the state. We also escorted various high-profile veterans around the state—such as General Wesley Clark and Senator Max Cleland. Not all veterans were supportive. I received an e-mail from one veteran that read: "Paratroopers are rolling over in their graves knowing that you're supporting John Kerry." It was the first—but not the last—time I would be attacked by my fellow veterans. I enjoyed the camaraderie, energy, and teamwork of a campaign—each pitching in where needed. It was analogous to the military: Everyone had the same goal but a different task, each pulling together where needed.

Senator Kerry always wanted to meet fellow veterans when he touched down at an airport or arrived at an event. He spent twenty or thirty minutes talking with each one, and I was able to spend a little time talking with him and his wife, Theresa Heinz Kerry. Senator Kerry's bond with veterans impressed me, as did Kerry's own service record. This was a man who had entered the U.S. Navy during his senior year at Yale in 1966 while the Vietnam War raged, and served on active duty honorably until 1970. On his second deployment to Vietnam, he volunteered to serve in one of the war's most dangerous jobs, as an officer in charge of Swift Boats, leading five-man crews on patrols into enemy-controlled areas. Kerry's crew was involved in three direct combat engagements, and he saved the life of one of his men, Special Forces Lieutenant Jim Rassmann, earning the Silver Star, Bronze Star, and three Purple Hearts. But despite his heroic service, and despite ten of eleven crewmates giving a testament to his valor and injuries, a group of Republican veterans calling themselves the Swift Boat Veterans for Truth attempted to tarnish the record of Lieutenant Kerry.

Bearing decades-old grudges that stemmed from Kerry's criticism of the Vietnam War when he returned home, these veterans used personal attacks and smears to sully his service record. To promote their agenda, they ran inaccurate and inflammatory television commercials, financed by wealthy Republicans who didn't seem to mind that President George W. Bush had avoided serving in Vietnam at all costs, or that Vice President Dick Cheney had supported the Vietnam War but received five deferments, saying, "I had other priorities in the sixties than military service."

That fall, the Swift Boaters, as they became known, were going on a national radio tour to broadcast their views, and the

Philadelphia Vietnam Veterans Memorial was their first stop. Fifteen minutes before the Swift Boaters' press conference was supposed to begin, someone tracked me down, asking me to get to the press conference as quickly as I could to speak on behalf of Senator Kerry. I didn't have any media training, but I didn't care. I planned to speak from the heart. To paraphrase the famous West Point cadet prayer, "Never be content with a half-truth when the whole can be won." I planned to win the whole truth.

As soon as their news conference ended, it was my turn. The reporters present had been alerted in advance by Mark Nevins, a bright twentysomething from Philadelphia, that I was an Iraq veteran who was there to defend Senator Kerry. One reporter asked, "As a veteran, how does it make you feel to see them attack John Kerry's military record?" Standing just a few feet away from where Patty Ward's name was etched in dark granite, I replied that it was a disgrace to have a press conference attacking another veteran's service, especially in the well of this Vietnam Veterans Memorial, a place that's supposed to be hallowed ground. "You wouldn't dishonor a church like that by holding a press conference on the altar, and then attack one of its members," I said.

"What do you know about war?" a local conservative radio talk show host interrupted, thinking he could bully me. When I told him respectfully that I actually knew quite a bit about war, having just returned from Iraq with the 82nd Airborne, he backed down. But at home that night, ironing my dress shirt for work the next day, I tuned in to his radio show only to hear his comments about this guy Patrick Murphy, some thirty-year-old from Northeast Philly who claims he got a Bronze Star in the army. "Claims"? Immediately, a listener called in, saying that I was too young to have served in Desert Storm and that I must be lying. Desert Storm? What were they talking about? The host knew I had just returned from Iraq. But instead of correcting the record, he let the lie stand. "You might be on to something," he said. That's how some folks in the media do it—they try to chip away at a person's honor, hoping a controversy will boost their ratings.

Not every Republican let the Swift Boaters' smears go unanswered—Senator John McCain, a Bush supporter and prisoner of war in Vietnam, stood strong. "I condemn the [Swift Boaters' television] ad. It is dishonest and dishonorable. As it is, none of these individuals served on the boat [Kerry] commanded. Many of his crewmates have testified to his courage under fire. I think John Kerry served honorably in Vietnam." The Swift Boaters were eventually fined $300,000 by the Federal Elections Commission in 2006. True patriots respect and honor a veteran's service, even if they do not agree with his politics. That should be nonnegotiable.

Unfortunately, it was not the last time a veteran's honor would be attacked.

•

That November, we overcame twenty-three visits by President Bush to put our swing state of Pennsylvania in the Democratic column. But President Bush remained in office—this time with what he called a "mandate." In Congress, Republicans stayed in power with incumbents trouncing their challengers by an average of forty points. Of the 400 sitting congressmen who sought reelection, 393 won. I knew it meant we would continue the same failed policies in Iraq.

The pundits piled on with interpretations and explanations. MSNBC analyst Chris Matthews called the Republican Party "the

Daddy Party" and the Democrats "the Mommy Party." Charlie Cook, a respected Washington political analyst, said, "Democrats run the risk of becoming perpetual losers, with a self-defeating mentality to match." Congressman Rahm Emanuel, head of the Democratic Congressional Campaign Committee, quietly told Minority Leader Nancy Pelosi in December 2004 that the Democrats could maybe win a couple of seats in 2006, but couldn't take the House back until 2008. The party's prospects were not promising.

•

When the campaign ended—and our attempt to influence the course of the war failed—I had to decide where I would live and what I would do. As a child in Northeast Philadelphia, I appreciated being able to walk two feet out my front door, knock on the front door of our same-step neighbors, the Rahns, and borrow a cup of milk for my Cheerios before school. But I had also come to love Bucks County. Starting from eighth grade through high school, I'd hop a car ride four or five times a week with my father, brother, or hockey teammates for a fifteen-minute drive to the Grundy Ice Rink, the home rink for Archbishop Ryan and other local high schools. Inside, the ice surface was surrounded by four-foot-high hockey boards and a chained fence instead of the usual, more expensive Plexiglas. This simple rink was set in a beautiful, old-time town called Bristol located right on the Delaware River in Bucks County. Memories of Bristol and later driving to Bucks County Community College through endless green pastures and farmland made me want to settle there.

When I transferred to King's College in 1992, my mother and father moved to the central Pennsylvania farmland near

Hershey. I enjoyed visiting—and even worked in the Reese's Factory before joining the army—but it wasn't home. Hershey was too far from my beloved Phillies, Flyers, Sixers, and Eagles, let alone cheesesteaks and soft pretzels. My mother, always quick with practical advice, weighed in that if I wasn't moving close to them in Hershey, then Bucks County was where I should move because it boasted one of the best school systems in the state—a fact she had learned working over the last decade for state senator Joe Conti, a moderate Republican. That's my mom—using her knowledge of local school systems to plan ahead for her grandchildren!

Bucks County it was. I found a great apartment in New Hope, just up the river from Washington Crossing, where General George Washington and his troops had crossed into Trenton, surprising the Hessians on Christmas Eve during the Revolutionary War. The apartment was attached to the home of Paul and Jan Witte, two community mainstays I had become friendly with during the 2004 campaign. Paul was an inventor who partnered with his wife, Jan, to establish the Hepatitis B Foundation. They lived on a street by the river, only a short three-minute walk from the restaurants, art galleries, and vibrant center of New Hope. I became so friendly with Paul and Jan that I'd often sit at their kitchen table and join them for breakfast or dinner. Legend has it that Albert Einstein used to play cards at that same table on visits from nearby Princeton University.

I also became active in the community, as I had done throughout college, law school, and the army, and frequently attended the local Catholic church. Soon, the dynamic pastor at St. Martin of Tours Church, Father Fred Kindon, asked me to join their Parish Counsel, which met every other week. I was also invited by Bishop McFadden—the number two official in the Archdiocese of Philadelphia and the brother of my first-grade teacher, Sister Jane McFadden—to serve on their Stewards Alliance, a group of young professionals offering support for special-needs schools in the archdiocese. In addition, with Easter Sunday on the horizon, I joined a Lenton Prayer group from St. Martin of Tours that met at a member's home in Washington Crossing.

Meanwhile, I was applying to several law firms. I had a couple thousand dollars in my savings account from my years in the army, but this soon dwindled and I had little left after rent and other necessities. I quickly focused on Cozen O'Connor, a top international law firm of 550 attorneys and 2,000 employees worldwide that was based in Philadelphia. I thought I was hired in December, then heard the position was filled, and was ultimately called back in February for several additional interviews. The final one was with named partner Patrick O'Connor, a King's College alum and the brother of my mentor, Mike O'Connor. He offered me a job.

Because I lived an hour away from the firm's Center City offices, I'd often leave my apartment by 6:00 a.m. Working with 250 other attorneys in the three-floored Philadelphia office, above the Philadelphia Stock Exchange, was certainly prestigious. The job also paid a lot better than any I had ever had, more than double my army salary. But it wasn't satisfying. Something was missing. And I would soon be pulled into public service again.

A Different Kind of Service

During those few months when I was working for John Kerry, speaking on college campuses and in VFW halls, at house parties and rallies, and meeting with local and statewide Democratic leaders, people began encouraging me to run for office. "You'd make a great candidate," they'd say, or "Patrick, we need more veterans in Congress." I was flattered, but focused on electing Senator Kerry. I had worked my tail off—eighteen- and nineteen-hour days were the norm—because I saw helping him get elected as the best way for me to help us change course in Iraq. But in the months after he lost, I began wondering whether the best way to help bring about that change was to run for Congress myself.

•

In Pennsylvania's Eighth Congressional District, which encompasses Bucks County, Northeast Philadelphia, and a small part of Montgomery County, Republican congressman Mike Fitzpatrick was up for reelection. He had been a rubber stamp for George Bush on Iraq and his defeat could have an impact on the war.

When I mentioned the possibility of running for office to friends from the Kerry campaign, one thought I was "crazy." Another asked how I could run with no money—a fair question. Another said I was "overreaching." When I sought advice from an influential Bucks County Democrat, I was told, after describing my background and interests in detail, "You've got a great story being a former professor at West Point and a Bronze Star in Iraq and all. But I have a great story, too. I graduated from Georgetown Law. You haven't paid your dues." It was a common refrain. Some felt I was just too young to run and should run for state representative first, but I couldn't have any say on our policy in Iraq in the state legislature, and that was what led me to enter the race. Others, especially my brother and close friends, were more encouraging. They felt my story was compelling, my heart was in the right place, and, I like to think, sensed that I wouldn't back down from what everyone knew would be an uphill fight.

Even as I continued to keep long hours practicing law, billing clients in six-minute increments, I also spoke to my family and asked their advice. My mom, cautious and always blunt, told me no, I shouldn't do it. I should focus on making partner at Cozen O'Connor and maybe run for office in five or ten years. My father told me that he'd support whatever I chose to do, but to do it well.

I also prayed about the decision with Kathy Gohl, a devout Catholic and Republican from Washington Crossing who hosted our weekly Lenten group. I told her how Bobby Kennedy had given hope to so many people because he felt an urgency to do what was right. When he finally ran for the presidency in 1968, Kennedy had said:

> I do not run . . . merely to oppose any man, but to propose new policies. I run because I am convinced that this country is on a perilous course and because I have such strong feelings about what must be done, and I feel that I'm obliged to do all I can.

I wasn't as good-looking, eloquent, or wealthy as RFK, but he expressed my own feelings perfectly.

Finally, in the spring of 2005, with my personal savings at $322, without a single campaign dollar in the bank, without anybody knowing who the hell I was, and with a working-class Northeast Philly accent that made the blue bloods in Pennsylvania politics cringe (an accent I'll probably have until the day I die), I decided to go for it. We had to put our country back on track, and impossible odds were not enough to deter me. As Captain Langley had said in Iraq, "Remember—impossible is our regular workday."

•

By Pennsylvania law, every county must have a county commissioner who's a member of the minority political party. Our minority county commissioner was a lifelong Democrat, Sandy Miller, a vibrant redhead and habitual smoker in her late fifties who was about to become the longest-serving Bucks County commissioner in history. I had met Commissioner Miller at an event for Senator Kerry months earlier. Now, I looked up her number on the Internet and gave her a ring. She agreed to meet me for lunch at a local restaurant called Goodnose. I confided my plans to her and she laid out the challenges I would face—and committed to support me on the spot. I was stunned. Tough as nails, deliberate, and thoughtful, she made a gut decision that I will never forget.

Next I went to see Chairman Robert A. "Bob" Brady, whom I called Congressman Brady, a barrel-chested, sixty-year-old former union carpenter, who serves as chairman of the Philadelphia Democratic Committee. When I met Chairman Brady for the first time, I was a little nervous. He ran the powerful Philadelphia Democratic machine and looked like he could still bench-press four hundred pounds easy. But when I mentioned I was the son of a Philadelphia police officer, Bob lit up like a Christmas tree, proudly showing me the badge his father had used when he was a cop on the job. The meeting lasted all of twenty minutes, and at the end he said, "You need to meet Jack Murtha."

Congressman John Murtha was a tough, no-nonsense, seventy-two-year-old retired marine colonel. A Korean War veteran and the first Vietnam combat veteran elected to Congress, Murtha had represented the people of Johnstown, Pennsylvania, for the past twenty years. Among veterans and many Pennsylvanians, he is a legend. When Congressman Brady set up the meeting, he gave me a warning: "Don't be late. Jack Murtha won't meet you if you're late."

I showed up thirty minutes early. Bob Brady arrived early, too. Colonel Murtha, unlike some politicians, came as advertised. He stands about 6'4" and shakes hands with what feels like a catcher's mitt. We sat down to talk, and when I told him I had been a paratrooper in the 82nd Airborne Division, he turned to Bob and asked incredulously, "Can you believe this guy jumped out of perfectly fine airplanes?" Over the next thirty minutes, I provided them with a rundown on why I was entering the race, and how I thought I could win. I also showed them an eight-page prospectus I had drafted with the help of a friend from Bucks County, Ed Haggerty. It had information about my life, the district, and how much money I planned to raise. I wasn't asking their permission to run, and they didn't make any promises of support. All I wanted was a chance, and I knew I had to earn it.

I also had a meeting with Congressman Rahm Emanuel, the national chairman of the Democratic Congressional Campaign Committee. Rahm is a hard-nosed political warrior in his mid-forties, who cut his teeth in Chicago politics and the Clinton White House; he is also the kind of guy who could probably make or break the career of someone in my position. I was excited about the meeting and gave him my eight-page prospectus. Rahm impatiently flipped through it and handed it back. "This is nice," he said. "But don't come back until you've raised $250,000." That was the last thing he said. The meeting lasted less than five minutes. It seemed he was either pissed off or didn't think I should be taken seriously. Twelve years earlier, when I joined the army, I had drill instructors at Fort Knox who would tear us down to build us back up. I wasn't sure how to take Rahm's dismissal, but it wasn't going to deter me.

A little while later, in May 2005, I made it official, announcing in a press release that I would enter the primary campaign. It even got a passing mention in the local newspaper.

•

At this point, I didn't even know what I didn't know about campaigns. But my politically astute brother, J.J., gave me a copy of the book *How to Win a Local Election*, and I devoured it. The book noted that there are over 537,000 elected offices in the United States, so I knew I didn't have to reinvent the wheel. I asked those who had been through the battles how to succeed. Most recommended hiring a finance director instead of a campaign manager. "Everyone hires a campaign manager first, but a candidate can run his own campaign in the beginning," they said, advising me that a campaign should be focused on raising money, not spending it. I took their advice and hired a finance director. Meanwhile, two college and two high school volunteers selflessly worked out of a donated basement office along the river in New Hope, getting our shoestring operation up and running. The office was a dusty, windowless storage space below a store; but it had one thing going for it: It was free (and filed as a campaign donation). So we put a fresh coat of paint on the walls and made the best of it. Besides, I told the team, working there built character. We had two old computers, two phone lines, and occasional visits by large rats that generously left their droppings.

After a local activist bailed as our campaign manager, I turned to a buddy, a former marine fighter pilot from Bucks County named Ed Jascewicz. Jas had been working as a pilot for United Airlines and lived with his wife and daughter in nearby Yardley. We had hit it off during the Kerry campaign, and soon he was acting not as our "campaign manager" but as our "executive officer." Jas didn't feel comfortable calling himself the campaign manager, because he had never run a campaign. He didn't even want a title. But we had to give him something so he could make it sound like he had authority and wasn't just a military buddy. In the military we have executive officers, so that's what Jas and I agreed to. It was pretty simple, Jas liked to say: He just provided a little adult supervision to the team when I was at work during the day. His new title was even reported in the local papers when he called up the *Philadelphia Daily News* columnist Stu Bykofsky and asked him if I could enter a local candidates' comedy night for charity. Jas got Stu's attention and I was added to the program. What we wouldn't do for a little free publicity.

•

By midsummer 2005, four Democratic candidates had entered the primary. Democrats have a reputation for infighting—a reputation that was about to be put to the test. There was Democratic activist Ginny Schrader, who had run and lost her campaign for the same seat two years earlier (a race I had seen firsthand while I was on the Kerry campaign). Ginny was a wonderful lady and a successful attorney, but not a strong campaigner. Prior to her sole 2004 debate against Mike Fitzpatrick, the national Republican Party sent out a direct mail flyer calling Ginny, a Jewish grandmother from Yardley, a supporter of Hezbollah. But rather than fight back, Ginny walked out of her debate with Mike Fitzpatrick when he wouldn't apologize. I had come to her defense against the Hezbollah allegations, but now she was my primary opponent and telling people I was too young to run for Congress—even though, at thirty-one, I was six years older than the constitutional age requirement.

Paul Lang was also a contender. A well-spoken and charismatic twenty-eight-year-old from Northampton, Bucks County, Paul was a part-time law and business student at the University of Maryland. During his time in the coast guard he had fallen into the Bering Sea and broken his back on a drug interdiction mission in Alaska. Hence his campaign slogan: "I broke my back for my country, and I'm willing to do it again for you." I respected Paul. He was a hard worker and looked you in the eye when he spoke to you.

Our other serious early primary opponent was Andy Warren, a sixty-two-year-old regional director of the Pennsylvania Department of Transportation and former fifteen-year Bucks County commissioner. He was well known and had the support of a powerful Democrat in the state senate. But Andy had a potentially fatal flaw as a primary candidate. He registered as a Democrat only recently—after the Republican machine passed over him to support Mike Fitzpatrick in 2004, to succeed Congressman Jim Greenwood, and passed over him again for Republican county commissioner. For many Democratic primary voters, this was a sign he wasn't someone they could trust to carry the Democratic banner.

There were also other potential candidates mentioned throughout the campaign. In a conversation with a particularly wealthy and influential prospect, I said, "If I lose in the primary against you, I won't be able to run for dogcatcher in this state, but I'm doing this for the nineteen guys I served with who never made it home." The national Democratic Party leadership thought this particular prospect was their best choice and tried to get Bob Brady to persuade me to withdraw. "This guy Patrick just served in Iraq," Bob told them. "I'm not asking him to do that. Have your candidate run against him!" Thankfully, that prospect decided not to run. Maybe it had to do with my passion or, more likely, the fact that we were door-knocking in ninety-degree heat in their neighborhood sixteen months before the general election.

One top state Democratic official summed up the race—and, at the same time, dismissed my chances—by saying: "Lang's got the best story. Warren's got the best Rolodex. Murphy's a nice guy." But that verdict started changing when we reported our fund-raising totals. I hate that money is so influential in politics. But the amount of money a campaign can raise is almost universally acknowledged as the key measure of its viability. In 2004, 98 percent of candidates who outraised their opponents won. So we dedicated ourselves to the task. Finding the time to raise money for the primary campaign was tough, since I was still working full-time at the law firm. Even asking people to contribute was difficult, though knowing it was helping us fight for change in Iraq made it easier.

For three to four hours every late afternoon—time I would have rather spent meeting voters—I'd sit and do "call time." Call time consisted of the finance director or a volunteer handing me sheets of paper with the names of local residents who had previously given to Democrats. I'd leave my office in downtown Philadelphia and walk over to Ellen Rose's co-op in Center City, Philadelphia, to make the calls. Ellen is sixty-nine years young, an intensely active retired women's studies professor who worked side by side with me as a full-time volunteer for Senator Kerry. She is a proud liberal, with a big heart and a sharp mind—and her cordless phone usually worked for about two hours a day before its battery ran out and I had to use my cell phone. Cramming into her one-bedroom apartment was not glamorous, especially because she thought air conditioners were a waste of electricity. But that's where we dedicated ourselves to the cause.

It was humbling when people gave time or money to our campaign, especially those who had so little to give. When a former neighbor in Northeast Philly, Mrs. Frances Nell, contributed $1,000, I couldn't believe it. She had never made a political contribution before and still lived in the row house across the street from where I grew up. Decades earlier, I had shoveled snow from her steps and helped her late husband, a navy veteran, get into his wheelchair. It was help like hers and the financial support of my family and friends that gave us a shot and kept me in the fight early on. By the time the quarter ended on June 30, 2005, we had raised $90,000—all in just six weeks. My opponents didn't come close. Paul Lang had roughly $22,000, nearly all of which was a personal loan; Andy Warren and Ginny Schrader didn't raise more than $5,000 each. Day after day throughout that summer, fall, and then winter, working full-time at Cozen O'Connor and somehow fitting call time into the daily schedule, we eventually hit $250,000—Rahm Emanuel's threshold for whether he'd be willing to talk to us again.

One reason we met this goal was our finance chair, Alan Sheriff. I first met Alan when he called me up out of the blue one day that summer and invited me to come to his home in Newtown. He was committed to bringing about change in this country and had focused his efforts on unseating Mike Fitzpatrick. He thought I might be the one to do it. Alan had worked on Wall Street for over twenty years, first climbing the ranks at Salomon Brothers and then becoming managing director at Credit Suisse First Boston. Retiring early, Alan moved with his wife, Karen, and their three sons from New York City to Bucks County. Alan has a compassionate heart, a tough business acumen, and, like my own brother, J.J., natural political instincts. Soon after that hour-long conversation, he joined our campaign. Barely a day has gone by since that Alan or I doesn't pick up the phone to discuss a newspaper article, sports trade, or recent political news. He is the older Jewish brother I never had.

Folks complain that there aren't enough genuine people involved in politics. They should meet Alan.

•

At Cozen O'Connor, I attended a firm reception for Democratic district attorney Lynn Abraham, my boss from my law school internship in 1997. Mayor Frank Rizzo had once referred to her as "one tough cookie," but I'll never forget her hugging me when the mother of the girl slain in the Carnival Killing wrote her a thank-you letter mentioning my help in prosecuting her daughter's killer.

I had planned to stop by the reception, just to say hello to Lynn and get back to my daily billable hours. But I decided to stick around when I noticed one of Lynn's aides. She was a knockout—blond and thin, with a smile that literally made me want to smile. With my heart racing and my mouth dry, I summoned the courage to approach her. As she turned toward me, introducing herself as Jenni Safford, all I could muster was an unoriginal "So where are you from?" She smiled and said, "Bucks County." I tried my hardest to respond with something imaginative but uttered a lame "You're a Democrat from Bucks County, too?" hoping she'd be impressed that I was also one of the few Democrats in our county. "No, I'm a Republican," she corrected me, and winked with one of her bright hazel eyes. I almost lost my breath. I noticed she had no wedding band or engagement ring and tried desperately to continue the conversation. "Oh, but I thought you worked for Lynn Abraham," I said, trying to understand why a Republican would work for a Democrat. "I don't work for Lynn. I thought you worked for Lynn. I'm a trusts and estates attorney here at Cozen O'Connor on the fourth floor."

After I told her I was in a different practice at Cozen and on the fifth floor, Jenni politely but abruptly excused herself. I didn't know what happened. She later confessed that she, too, had felt a spark and sensed our conversation could go somewhere but had a strict policy of not dating anyone at work. I had been back from Iraq for over a year now, and ever since my broken engagement, I had been shy around women. But when I saw her a couple of weeks later at another firm reception, I again got up the courage to walk over to her. "How's my favorite Democrat from Bucks County?" she said, winking at me again. I knew I wanted to ask her out. With the smoothness of industrial-size sandpaper, I replied, "I'm great. Hey, I really enjoyed our conversation the other day. Would you like to go out sometime, maybe Friday?" "No, I'm busy, sorry." "Saturday?" I said, my face crunching like I was about to get a needle in the arm. "I can't." I made one last attempt: "How about Sunday? I can take you out for a Rita's Water Ice. You like water ice, don't you?" Rita's is a regional favorite that I was hoping she couldn't resist. "Yes. I guess I can," she said. I was ecstatic.

After picking her up that Sunday afternoon and immediately confessing that I had debated at length how casually I should dress, we went to Rita's Water Ice on South Street, ordered one cherry and one lemon water ice, and walked along the Delaware River in downtown Philadelphia. It was a beautiful day and I barely noticed the three hours pass. I was hooked on Jenni like I could never have imagined. She had everything I had always dreamed of: brains, looks, personality, strength of character—and she even laughed at my jokes.

When I dropped her off early in the evening to go back to work at the firm and catch up on some billable hours, my heart was still racing. I called Chris Norbeck and couldn't hide how

I felt. I told him something I had never said before: "I just met the one." I admired Jenni. She had earned her way to the top of one of the best law firms in the country. She had grown up in a broken home, often taking care of her two younger siblings, and helping pay her way through college by working with autistic children at a local YMCA. She had also earned a juris doctorate and master's degree in business administration from Temple University where, she needles me still, I was wait-listed for law school.

Our first official night date was the following Thursday and, fittingly, at an event for local Democratic candidates in Bucks County—a performance of the show *Chicago* at the local Quakertown playhouse. The local Democratic chair, Bill Brousis, must have known I was crazy about Jenni, because he gave me the two front seats that had been saved for Pennsylvania governor Ed Rendell, who hadn't been able to attend.

Falling in love with Jenni grounded me during that busy time. I was working almost twenty hours a day, and Jenni gently and frequently reminded me that I didn't have to win the congressional race all in one day. Jenni was more cautious early in the relationship, but eventually she admitted she was falling for me as well. Besides my kindness and terrible jokes, what stood out to her, she said, was that I was "gritty." It was the first time I ever heard that word used as a romantic compliment. But I was (and am) way out of my league with her—so if she wants to call me gritty, I'm okay with that.

•

One of the turning points in the primary campaign came in August, during a candidates' forum with top Philadelphia Internet bloggers at Yard's Brewery. The forum was moderated by Chris

Bowers of MyDD.com, a huge supporter of Ginny Schrader. I hadn't been invited, but as an avid reader of MyDD.com and other local political blogs, I decided just to show up. Unlike the other candidates, I didn't have campaign materials or prepared remarks, but when I explained who I was, I was invited to give a brief speech.

I told the packed crowd what it was like to drive in 138-degree heat in a Humvee without doors while looking out for hidden IEDs on the side of the road. I told them why I believed we needed to fight for a change of course in Iraq. In a community growing tired of a mismanaged war and hungry for candidates with the national security credibility to take on the no-holds-barred GOP machine, a fire was lit. After the session, bloggers posted entries like this from the Tattered Coat: "It's so gratifying to see that soldiers like . . . Patrick Murphy have come back from Iraq, and are now speaking out about what they saw and taking part in the political process." The buzz from the netroots community gave our team hope during those early days, and helped us get taken seriously.

While the forum at Yard's Brewery and falling in love with Jenni were the high points during the summer of 2005, my appearance on Chris Matthews's *Hardball* was a low point. In August, in the middle of a busy day of work and three hours of call time, an MSNBC producer gave me a ring, asking if I could come down to the studio later that day to be a guest on the show. It was my first national television appearance, and I was confident, expecting to talk about the future. But Chris relentlessly asked me about the past.

> MATTHEWS: If you were in Congress back in 2002, right before that last congressional election . . . when

> they decided to go to war or not, would you have voted authorizing going to war in Iraq?

My mind immediately raced to the nineteen paratroopers who didn't make it home. Would my answer tarnish their memory if I said no? There was no time to digest the question on Chris's fast-paced show.

> Me: That's a tough question. It is hard to play Monday morning quarterback. . . .
>
> Matthews: Patrick, you would have voted nay, then?

I tried again, but I couldn't get a clear answer out:

> Me: I would have made sure.
>
> Matthews, cutting me off: You have to vote—let me tell you how Congress . . . I'm not going to talk to you like this. I was going to be sarcastic, but I thank you for your service, so I'll treat you with respect. You have to vote aye or nay. Would you have voted aye to go to war or nay not to?
>
> Me: It's a hard call, Chris.
>
> Matthews, cutting me off: I know. That's why you run for Congress. You shouldn't run for Congress if you don't want to make that call. You have two years. You can look back and decide whether it was the right way to vote. Those guys who had to

> vote then had to look ahead. You're looking back. Was it a right or wrong vote to authorize going into Iraq?

I felt like a rookie trying to swing at Roger Clemens's fastballs. I was in the box, but just couldn't get my bat around fast enough.

> Me: It is hard to say.

> Matthews, cutting me off: No, it's not hard to say. You have three years of looking back. . . . So you're running for Congress and you're running on the war issue, but you're not saying whether you would have voted for authorizing the war or not.

> Me: Chris, you've got to understand, I served where nineteen guys lost their lives . . . I don't want to dishonor the guys I served with over there. So I am not going to say that.

Finally, a connection. "I understand that," Chris said, before taking me down another line of questioning. They call it *Hardball* for a reason, and I knew it was not a good interview for me. I should have spoken more aggressively, even over him, to get my point across. It was an honest response, but definitely not a strong one. I was still struggling with how to be a candidate after being a soldier for so long, how to be loyal to my fallen comrades while expressing my disapproval of the Iraq War.

I would not have voted to authorize the Iraq War. Iraq was not a threat or danger to the United States, hadn't attacked us on 9/11, and hadn't even had weapons of mass destruction, the primary justification for the war. There is no more important and vital constitutional responsibility than for the United States Congress to declare war. I believe I would have stood firm and had the courage to challenge what the Bush administration was trying to sell Congress and the American people. But at the time, I was a soldier expected to execute the foreign policies given to us by Washington, D.C., not to vote on or draft those policies.

Do I believe Saddam Hussein was a good man? No, he was a criminal and I'm glad he was brought to justice. But I just don't believe the United States needed to deploy 148,000 troops to Iraq in 2003 to depose him, especially because it took our eye off our true enemies, Osama bin Laden and al Qaeda, who were responsible for killing 2,974 innocent American civilians on 9/11, including Michele Hoffmann and eighteen residents of Bucks County. Today, the critical threat to America comes from these same criminals, who are camped out in the mountains of Afghanistan and the borders of Pakistan, plotting their next strike. And yet under President Bush our attention wrongly remains on Iraq.

●

The whole campaign was a baptism by fire. Every kind of attack was leveled at me. My stammering Chris Matthews interview was used in a negative ad. Because I had been single when I moved to New Hope, where there was a large gay community, my opponents began whispering that I was gay. Because the row house I grew up in was a couple hundred feet outside the Eighth Congressional District, maybe two city blocks, I was accused of being a carpetbagger, even though my apartment, some relatives, my grade school, church, hockey rink, and community college were all located within the district. Because I had voted for George W. Bush by military absentee ballot in 2000, having been duped by his "compassionate conservative" agenda, I was accused of not being a real Democrat. Because I didn't vote in the primary and general election every year, or even in the majority of elections since I had reached voting age, I was accused of not being a good citizen. Because I was pro-choice, I was accused of being a bad Catholic. Because I was Catholic, I was accused of not being pro-choice. The attacks were surreal. Sometimes I wondered what I had gotten myself into.

Opposing Democrats even stooped to slandering my service record, submitting letters to the editor in local papers claiming I wasn't a paratrooper in Iraq, just a claims adjuster. Ginny Schrader wrote an op-ed titled, "Service in Iraq Is Not Preparation for Service in Congress." Thankfully, Jon Soltz and the Iraq and Afghanistan Veterans of America came to my defense, as did most of the local netroots community. Such attacks were inexcusable.

But I never went negative on the irrelevant mistakes of my fellow Democrats. We could and did disagree publicly on policy differences, but as a regular citizen and a proud Democrat, I didn't like it when Democrats attacked each other on insignificant issues. And as a candidate, I tried not to, even though I was sometimes itching to criticize another candidate who I felt was being particularly hypocritical or self-aggrandizing.

Meanwhile, Jenni and I started to get serious very quickly. Both in our thirties, we had been through the tribulations of previous relationships. We both knew we were starting something truly special. While I loved New Hope, it was too expensive to buy a home there. Jenni and I often talked about our dream house, along the river, and raising our children in a safe environment with good schools. We didn't talk about it without blushing or hedging, but we talked about it.

One Saturday afternoon that fall we were driving down Radcliffe Street, a tree-lined road that runs along the Delaware River near the hockey rink I grew up playing on. Jenni and I saw a beautiful, redbrick Colonial home with a "For Sale" sign on it. It was a cloudless Saturday afternoon, and we were driving to a picnic in nearby Bristol, given by the Ancient Order of the Hibernians, a Catholic fraternal group I proudly belong to. But I immediately pulled to the shoulder of the road. As Jenni called the phone number on the sign, I jumped out of the car, walked up the driveway, and was halfway to the house before Jenni yelled, "You just can't knock on their door. You have to make an appointment through their Realtor."

I had never bought a home, but I knew I loved the place and wanted to see it right away. Jenni was embarrassed, but came up behind me to see if anyone would answer. We were given a tour by the owner, Mrs. Avis Anderson, a lovely local school nurse who was about to retire with her husband and move into something smaller. The home was cozy and immaculate, but the good omen that caught my eye was the Clinton-Gore mug in her kitchen. "So I see you're a Clinton fan?" I asked Avis with a smile. Blushing, she said, "Yeah, I may be one of the only Democrats in the area." I told her not to worry, she was among friends. We signed the paperwork and moved in a few months later.

•

My plan was to ask Jenni's hand in marriage after Midnight Mass on Christmas Eve, outside St. Mark's Catholic Church in

Bristol. I had arranged for an engagement ring to be shipped from Rudy's Jewelers in Fayetteville, North Carolina, where army paratroopers get a special discount on diamonds. In my haste to propose I had overlooked one critical detail: The Mass I took her to was in Spanish! We giggled as we tried to sing along to "Silent Night." After Mass, we walked outside, and I bent down on one knee, promising I would love her forever. Jenni said yes and started crying.

That same holiday season, I was approached by a political kingmaker in Pennsylvania with an offer I didn't expect: How would I like to be a Pennsylvania state representative, making over $65,000 a year with benefits, while being able to keep my job and nice paycheck at Cozen O'Connor, and not even face a primary? He said my chances were slim to win the congressional general election against Mike Fitzpatrick, "maybe three percent—so why don't you take the sure thing while you can?" My quick answer: a resounding "no." This type of backroom deal was undemocratic and made me uncomfortable. What's more, it was probably made just to take my temperature to see how much fight I had in me. The experts may have had me at 3 percent, but if my opponents were trying to cut a deal, they must not have felt so lucky.

•

Our primary campaign team was a tight-knit family, organized by department—finance, led by Tim Persico, a recent college grad who had a pale complexion and dark, curly hair and bore an uncanny resemblance to Congressman Mike Fitzpatrick; field, which organized door-knocking and phone-banking and included twenty-four-year-old Madeleine "Mads" Wille; and communications, run by Dan DeRosa and his sidekick Nate Hake. Josh Nanberg, a friend from the Kerry campaign, guided them and was known for drafting one of the shortest press releases in American politics. When Josh learned that a primary opponent had been endorsed by a local attorney who wasn't even an elected official, he responded with a concise "Okay."

We all worked out of our new headquarters on Edgely Road in Bristol Township. The space was owned by our campaign treasurer, Vanya Teryll, a fiftysomething accountant who loved Democratic politics even more than her beloved Philadelphia Eagles. When we moved into our new office, it was cluttered with old bags of potato chips, walls without drywall, and a six-foot-high green Canada Dry refrigerator that had mold caked all over its inside.

As each day brought us closer to the primary's Election Day, our office attracted growing numbers of volunteers—from our sixth grader Theresa Russo to our seventy-two-year-old WWII veteran Isadore "Izzy" Brosbe. It was a bare-bones base of operation. We handed out campaign literature printed on card stock because we didn't want to spend money on expensive glossy paper; our printer had to be manually fed one sheet of paper at a time. But we cleaned up the space, and it became a humming, if cramped, headquarters. For a while, it seemed like the only press interested in us was a Japanese crew, who followed us around because they were intrigued that a soldier was running for political office. Their cameramen created a buzz, but their coverage didn't exactly have a wide reach in the Philadelphia media market. When we eventually had visitors like ABC's George Stephanopoulos, we could sense that their teams felt slightly uncomfortable in our "interesting" campaign accommodations. Considering we'd just come from a rat-infested basement, I thought it was progress.

•

By the time the Bucks County Democratic Party held its endorsing conference in March 2006, Paul Lang and Ginny Schrader had dropped out to run for separate state senate seats. That left Andy, me, and another candidate who had declared late that spring, Fred Viskovich. Fred was a former partner at PricewaterhouseCoopers, who also wanted to get our troops home from Iraq and commanded a small bloc of voters. The night before the conference, I got a call from Wayne Kenton, a Democratic activist and one of my earliest supporters. He told me to ask Fred for his endorsement. That night, at a diner on Route 13, I did. We agreed on a plan.

When we showed up the next day at Richboro Middle School, where hundreds of Democratic activists were gathered for their endorsement meeting, the atmosphere was electric. When I rose to speak I sensed a connection with the crowd, many of whom had heard me speak before in smaller settings. When Fred took the floor, his booming voice resounded throughout the hall. "This race is too important for Democrats to beat each other up. We need to bring our troops home from Iraq," he said. "I've got thousands of signatures supporting my candidacy, but I'm forgoing my campaign so I can endorse your next congressman, Patrick Murphy." The place went wild. By the time Andy Warren spoke, not even Notre Dame's Knute Rockne could have turned the crowd in that room.

The night before, volunteers had driven around Bucks County in the heavy snow handing out campaign DVDs at the homes of Democratic committee members. In the previous months, I'd spoken at least once to each of Bucks County's several dozen local Democratic clubs and called each of its 435 committeemen to ask for their support. We had earned the party's endorsement with hard work. But it was Fred's support that sealed the deal. We were on our way.

•

In the run-up to primary Election Day, I took two weeks' vacation from Cozen O'Connor to work full-time on the campaign. The days began at about 5:00 a.m., when I ran a few miles with Tim Persico and Daren Berringer, a campaign consultant. At 5:45 a.m., Seth Frotman would meet me at my home. A twenty-five-year-old, sandy-haired dynamo who had graduated second in his law school class at Indiana University, Seth somehow averaged sixty hours a week as our researcher; sleep was a luxury he often went without. Nearly every morning, he'd be waiting for me with a cup of coffee and doughnut from the local Wawa convenience store. We were now finally getting limited but much-needed media coverage from our local papers in the *Bucks County Courier Times*, *Doylestown Intelligencer, Allentown Morning Call,* and *Philadelphia Inquirer,* which I read as he drove us to train stations throughout the district to greet commuters on the 6:15 a.m. trains. We'd stand there and talk with folks for about an hour and a half, whether it was sunny or a torrential downpour. Later in the fall, we'd even be out there in the bone-chilling cold. Countless commuters told us they'd never seen a candidate at a train station once, much less three or four times. It got to the point where SEPTA conductors recognized me and cheered me on as their trains pulled away.

After the train stations, we'd stop by the local diners for the breakfast crowd, shaking their hands as they ate while trying not to bother them. We'd then go to the campaign office to "start the day" with call time. Tim Persico and I sat at a folding table for hours on end. Tim would hand me the call sheet, with the person's name and number on each, and I'd dial. Most times we couldn't get through. Sometimes our intended callee wouldn't be in, sometimes they'd be "in a meeting." Sometimes I'd call a dozen or more times, but they were always "in a meeting." Each time, I'd leave a polite message, but it was frustrating. I had to check my ego at the door and focus on the task at hand. The only time Tim let me get up was if I had to use the bathroom. It was tiresome but critical work. Fitzpatrick had raised over $1 million more than I had at this point. If we wanted to win the primary and be competitive in the general election, we needed to make those crucial calls.

When I was finally released from call time, we'd stop by senior centers, Democratic Party events, or environmental groups, attending events and visiting diners late into the night. I loved meeting folks on the campaign trail; it's what I believe campaigns are all about. At the end of each day en route back to the campaign headquarters, usually about 11:00 p.m. or midnight, I'd ask to drive by Andy Warren's headquarters, only twenty minutes from ours. It was my way of seeing if we were working hard enough. The lights were usually off in his office. When we returned to our headquarters, pizza boxes or Chinese food would be strewn across collapsable tables; our team was still active, some folding letters, others addressing envelopes. It was a twenty-hours-a-day operation. The only time we shut down was when the second major flood happened within the year along the Delaware River and we sent our team to help with flood relief by assisting the local Red Cross. Flood relief is an issue that's been important to me since my days at King's College, and today, as a congressman, I'm fighting to make it easier for folks affected by floods to get the help they need.

•

Anyone involved in political campaigns will tell you that elections are family affairs. Jenni was my secret weapon. If we hadn't met, I would not have won—it's as simple as that. She gave me a lot of support—usually lovingly—but occasionally with a swift kick in the pants when I needed it. For our campaign, she sacrificed our "date nights," sitting down for meals, and spending time together planning our wedding. Jenni is strong-willed and intelligent, and I can still remember her forcefully sending an e-mail to our campaign team, explaining that while they might be reluctant to release "tentative" schedules to the public, she was an exception and was entitled to see them because they "tentatively" affected her life.

In addition to Jenni, my family and especially my brother, J.J., always came through. Each of them took a week's vacation to join our campaign full-time in the final stretch, and my parents and sister were there in the last few days, stuffing envelopes, making telephone calls, and door-knocking well after dark. But there were times I could not be there for them. When J.J. and his family moved into their new home in Wilkes-Barre, I couldn't make the two-hour drive to help them move in, like he had helped me move to Fort Bragg three years earlier. J.J. and my whole family understood that I was now in the whirlwind of a campaign. We had talked about these moments before I decided to run, but now when I reluctantly had to tell my brother I could not be there or had to decline my attendance at a niece's birthday party, I could sense a trace of disappointment on the other end of the phone. I had a close-knit family that was always there for one another, and it hurt not being there at every family gathering.

•

As we neared my first Election Day, I knew we were outworking and outthinking our opponent, Andy Warren, but I still wasn't certain it would be enough to beat someone with decades of Bucks County government experience. On Primary Election Day, May 16, 2006, I was at the Cornwells Heights train station early, greeting passengers on the platform on their way to work and encouraging them to vote. Later that morning, Jenni and I voted near our home. Everyone in my family then made their way to different polling places throughout Bucks County. That afternoon, Jenni and I had lunch at Chambers Restaurant in Doylestown to thank Dick Doran and Norval Reece, two senior Pennsylvania political pros who had come out of political retirement to help. I was restless and could barely finish my plate. I felt confident but didn't know whether my confidence was justified. I hated the feeling that there was nothing more I could do. In hockey, I could always make the extra effort to make a play on the ice; in the army, I could always make one last check on my men and our mission status; but now, I had to be content with what we had done. Thankfully, Jenni was with me for most of the day, smiling and holding my hand, which also helped keep me sane.

Everyone on our campaign team was busy getting out the vote. As the polls closed and the last voters made their choice, Jenni and I went home to rest and await the results. The returns were coming in by phone and on television. By the time the nightly news was over, they were calling us the projected winner with a two-to-one margin. We had accomplished what many had thought impossible a year earlier. I was the Democratic nominee for United States Congress in Pennsylvania's Eighth District. Flanked by Jenni and my family at Georgine's Restaurant in Bristol Township, I thanked

Andy Warren for a spirited campaign, and focused our team on the fight ahead. With our last ounces of energy, we celebrated for a few hours.

The next day we drove to the train station to thank the voters for their support. The general election battle had begun.

Untouchable

When I voted at 10:00 a.m. on Primary Election Day, the incumbent, Republican congressman Mike Fitzpatrick, had some volunteers hold up one of his campaign signs behind me as I was being interviewed on television. Knowing his signs were there, I smiled to the cameras but gritted my teeth.

That night, when it was clear I had won, Fitzpatrick released a statement:

> I'd like to congratulate Pat Murphy on his nomination. . . . The voters now have a clear choice between Pat Murphy, a "cut and run" liberal, and me, Mike Fitzpatrick, a proven independent leader who knows we need a new plan for success in Iraq—and calls for an independent commission to develop it—but who won't risk our families' security by cutting and running.

Fitzpatrick was not going to yield an inch. I knew that if we were going to be successful, we needed to make some minor changes to our team. Months earlier, during a time when fundraising wasn't particularly fruitful, a staff member on the campaign laughingly replied out of my earshot to the question of how we're doing, "At least we made payroll." When I heard this report from my brother, I was hurt and embarrassed. To this staffer, I felt, our campaign for Congress was, at the end of the day, a paycheck. For me and most of the others, it was a calling.

I had let him know I wasn't happy, even giving the "this is my last warning" speech several times during the primary. But I'm a loyal person, and had tossed and turned for a week, unable to sleep soundly even after the primary win. I talked it over with Alan Sheriff, and J.J., and Jenni. From my military training, I knew I needed to make the tough call—I was ultimately responsible for everything our team accomplished, or failed to accomplish. In the end, I needed every team member completely committed to our cause. So I let him go. As General Patton once said, "I'd rather have a loyal staff officer than a brilliant one." When word got out, some political insiders chafed at my decision, even confronting me at political events. But I stood by it.

We didn't have a lot of money to spend on our staff but, with the Democratic nomination in a potentially top congressional race, I was confident we could recruit top campaign talent. Alan took two weeks off work to identify prospects, and after dozens of résumés and calls, I zeroed in on Scott Fairchild. Scott had made his mark in Virginia, where he had helped Democratic governor Tim Kaine win in a Republican stronghold. I liked him right off the bat. He had been a waiter, cook, and supervisor at a Friendly's restaurant, and was a straight shooter, someone who wasn't in politics to schmooze or meet powerful people or advance his own agenda.

He commented during his interview at Alan's New Hope office, when I asked him why he wanted to be my campaign manager, "The way I can best serve my country is to help elect people to turn things around." He gave another memorable answer when we said we weren't sure how much we could pay him. "Money's not important—I just want to beat Republicans." Direct, full of conviction, and combative—I liked Scott immediately. It also helped that Jenni thought he was great. When we took him out to dinner after the job interview at Anabella's, Jenni's favorite Italian restaurant in Bristol, Jenni didn't finish her meal and asked if Scott would like the rest. He polished it off without blushing.

Scott was so tireless in his work for the campaign that he allowed an ear infection to get worse because he didn't want to take time off to get it checked out. As a result, I walked in on him one day self-medicating in the bathroom of our campaign office as our new communications director Carrie James poured peroxide into his ear. I wasn't the only one who noted Scott's "zeal." When James Carville, President Clinton's former campaign manager, did an event for us a few months after Scott arrived, he and Scott had a chance to talk. As Ben Mundel, one of our bright and talented UPenn supervolunteers, drove Carville back to the Philadelphia airport, Carville, the Ragin' Cajun himself, said without prompting, "That guy Scott's crazy—you guys are gonna do just fine."

As we built our A team, Carrie was one of our best new hires. A graduate of Gettysburg College, Carrie had been working in the office of then minority leader Nancy Pelosi. Congressman Rahm Emanuel got her and some of the best and brightest

Democratic staffers in Washington in a room and told them they needed to get out of Washington and into the field to help bring our Democratic candidates to victory. So Carrie left the confines of the leader's office to live in a twin bed in the home of Bristol Township councilwoman Tina Davis, who graciously loaned her a mammoth red pickup truck with tires bigger than she was.

Like a football team, a campaign needs a good air game—TV and radio ads—and a good ground game—fieldwork—to build grassroots support. So we expanded our offensive line to five field coordinators that summer: Doug Platz, in conservative Quakertown; Sara Schaumburg, in Southeast Bucks County; Nat Binns, in Central Bucks; in south central, Brendan Flynn; and, in my old neighborhood of Northeast Philly, Ben Grossberg.

It was just the sort of team I needed to take on Mike Fitzpatrick and the Republican machine. Born and raised in Bucks County, Fitzpatrick attended a conservative college in Florida before going to Dickinson law school, where he was classmates with Rick Santorum, the right-wing Pennsylvania senator. Before getting elected to Congress, Fitzpatrick had served as a popular county commissioner for ten years. To most residents and political "experts," Fitzpatrick seemed untouchable, his reelection a foregone conclusion, especially considering he had won his 2004 race by a whopping twelve-point margin, equal to over fifty thousand more votes. Further, large swaths of the state were a Republican stronghold, including Bucks County. In fact, the GOP held eight of the ten state representative seats, four of the state senate seats, the U.S. congressional seat, and majority control of most of the local school boards and supervisor seats in Bucks County. Fitzpatrick also had a campaign bank account well over seven figures, was known as a tireless campaigner at age forty-one, and was a freshman congressman in the Republican majority party, a majority his party wanted desperately to keep.

That spring, polling by Jef Pollock's Global Strategy Group showed Fitzpatrick was as popular in Bucks County, which is about 90 percent of the district, as President Bill Clinton. Of likely voters, 49 percent were Republican, only 38 percent were Democratic, and 57 percent of them gave Fitzpatrick a favorable job approval rating. In general, political scientists say that anyone with a job approval rating over 55 percent is a shoo-in for reelection. When we started, Fitzpatrick was roughly twenty points ahead in the polls. "If you don't win," I was told repeatedly, "don't let it dampen your interest in politics." Even Jenni's grandmother Vicky Martin—Mrs. Martin to me—said, "You know, I hear you have a bright future if you don't win this one."

But never underestimate the will of a paratrooper. In June 1944, at the height of World War II, American paratroopers in Normandy conducted the most ambitious airborne operation ever. During thirty-three days of bloody combat, the 82nd Airborne Division had 5,245 paratroopers killed, wounded, or missing. They were led by Major General James "Slim Jim" Gavin the youngest American two-star general since the Civil War. Less than six months later, the 82nd Airborne, a light infantry unit, reinforced an American tank division that was repelling a German offensive in the Battle of the Bulge in the Ardennes Forest. In one of the greatest moments in military history, an 82nd Airborne paratrooper, Private First Class Martin, with just the weapons on his back, called to a retreating tank destroyer sergeant from the foxhole he was digging: "Are you looking for a safe place? Well, buddy . . . pull your vehicle behind me—I'm the 82nd Airborne, and this is as far as the bastards are going!" The Allied Forces beat back the German offensive and went on to win the most costly battle in the war, losing over eighteen thousand American lives. Even in the face of impossible odds, paratroopers come through. This was the warrior spirit ingrained in me and in our campaign. There was not a day that went by that I didn't believe we were going to win.

But it wasn't easy. Over the course of his one term in office, Fitzpatrick had done a good job of solidifying his relationships with the power players in the district. When I met with most unions, a traditional Democratic base in suburban Philly elections, they told me that Fitzpatrick was good for them. "What do you mean?" I asked, pointing out that he voted against their interests in Congress by opposing increases in the minimum wage and unfair trade deals like the Central American Free Trade Agreement (CAFTA). "He's loyal and takes our calls," they'd say, "so we can't back you."

Even the unions and organizations that I would have expected to be favorably inclined toward me were not. I'm a lifetime member of the Veterans of Foreign Wars, and Pop-Pop was a VFW post commander, and although my local post in Bristol Township supported me, the national VFW endorsed Fitzpatrick, who was not a veteran. Even though I was a former prosecutor, and my father, uncle Joe, and cousins were cops, and Fitzpatrick had voted to cut funding for the COPS program, which put more police officers on the streets, the Fraternal Order of Police supported Fitzpatrick.

But whenever it became clear that an organization or union I was meeting with wouldn't support me, I'd always say the same thing: "I'm going to win this race and I'm going to fight for you regardless. I just wish you were with me now." I wanted them to know that this wasn't quid pro quo, I'd still be on their side—I wouldn't abandon them just because they didn't support me. Other candidates took a different approach, bullying or threatening organizations that didn't endorse them. But in my view, I was running to represent the interests of everyone in my district, even those who didn't support me.

However, despite Fitzpatrick's and the GOP's grip on the district, I sensed there were vulnerabilities. On a number of issues, while Fitzpatrick stuck with the status quo, I offered fundamental change. On Iraq, the political analysts' advice was clear—attack Bush and Fitzpatrick for their incompetence in handling the war, but do not offer your own plan for Iraq. I felt that was exactly what was wrong with politics. People are tired of candidates who just complain and focus on why their opponent should be fired. I was going to lead a campaign that acknowledged our opponent's shortcomings but talked about why we should be hired. I'd refer to my proposals as Murphy Plans.

The Murphy Plan for Iraq called for a twelve-month timeline to redeploy our troops home, with a strategic strike force to train the Iraqis and go after al Qaeda where they were hiding, in the mountains of Afghanistan. This was a dramatic reduction of our footprint, and a necessary change in strategy. Our men and women serving honorably in Iraq would no longer be forced to stand in the middle of a religious civil war leading convoys up and down Ambush Alley and waiting to be hit by roadside bombs. The plan also called for Don Rumsfeld to be fired and for America to lead a surge in diplomacy, both inside Iraq and with the other countries in the region. Fitzpatrick called me "cut and run" and "irresponsible," but he never said what he would do differently.

One of the people who publicly endorsed our position on

Iraq was Kevin Emore, a field artillery officer with the 1st Armored Division. Kevin grew up in Northeast Philly and even played hockey for Archbishop Ryan before attending West Point, where he was one of my students. He was back from Iraq on a brief leave before returning and he wanted to attend a campaign press conference to help make the case that we needed a timetable to redeploy our troops and finally put pressure on the Iraqis to stand up. It was clearly against army regulations to participate in a political press conference. But when I warned him about it, prior to the event, he smiled and said: "What are they gonna do—send me back to Iraq?"

To help veterans, I offered a Murphy Plan for a 21st Century GI Bill of Rights, a dramatic increase in benefits focusing on education and home loans. It also called for stopping personnel policies such as the "backdoor" draft, which forced troops who signed up for three- or four-year tours after September 11, 2001, to stay in the military even after their initial commitments expired.

But I also knew that to earn voters' trust, I could not run entirely on what I would do to turn around the war or to help our men and women in uniform. I also had a responsibility to inform voters about what I would do to address their other concerns, including a scandal-plagued Washington. This is why I proposed a Murphy Plan on Ethics to end the Washington system that let congressmen take jobs as lobbyists the day after they left office. It called for a two-year cooling-off period and also banned gifts, meals, and travel subsidized by lobbyists.

I also took on the issue of embryonic stem cell research—research that offers hope for breakthroughs in treating Parkinson's disease, Alzheimer's disease, and spinal cord injury. The issue was important to me, but I gained a deeper appreciation for it after meeting Shelbie Oppenheimer. Shelbie and Jeff Oppenheimer were a couple in their late twenties when their family doctor diagnosed Shelbie with Lou Gehrrig's disease, a fatal condition with a life expectancy of only three to five years. Jeff and Shelbie broke down right in the doctor's office. But, eventually, they found strength in each other and vowed to fight the disease together. Now, a remarkable ten years later, Shelbie is still fighting.

I met Shelbie one day in the summer of 2006 in her living room, where she was now mostly confined to a hospital bed. She breathed through a ventilator and was able to speak softly without the ventilator for only twenty minutes a day. I sat at the edge of her bed, feeling comfortable enough after just a few minutes to hold her frail hand. She told me her story, about how she and Jeff had always wanted to be parents, and had adopted a beautiful little girl named Isabella, who was now eight years old. Shelbie tugged on my hand and said faintly, "Come closer." I leaned toward her, trying not to knock into any of the tubes or wires. My face was about twelve inches away from hers. "My voice isn't strong anymore," she said, pausing. "All I want out of life is to see Isabella go to her senior prom in ten years." She took another deliberate pause. "My only chance is through embryonic stem cell research. Do you support that?" Her eyes looked up at me, full of hope. "Yes, Shelbie, I do." Shelbie strained to smile. Tears formed in her eyes and started trickling down the side of her face. "Then I want you to tell my story. My voice is too soft, but yours is not." I was filled with emotion. Here is this young mother on what some might consider her deathbed, battling with every ounce of her energy, and she wanted me to champion her cause, even if she would not be alive to benefit from our efforts. I'm not sure I ever met anyone so selfless, so giving, and so brave.

For the rest of the campaign, we shared Shelbie's story with everyone who cared to listen. When Fitzpatrick was quoted in the press saying that all I talked about was stem cell research, I was proud.

•

Meanwhile, Jenni and I received the most unexpected and wonderful news: We were going to have a child. While we had been engaged for months and were considering dates for our wedding, we had now decided to get married on June 17, 2006, right after our primary win. Jenni had always dreamed of getting married on the beach in front of her grandparents' property, in Highland Beach, Florida, so that's what we did. A small gathering of friends and family witnessed the ceremony. My brother, J.J., served as my best man and Jenni's sister, Chrissy, was her maid of honor. Seeing Jenni dressed in white, walking down the beach, is a vision that still brings a smile to my face. We were able to take only a couple days off for the wedding, and three full days for our honeymoon in the British Virgin Islands, but the time away from the stressful and combative campaign was welcome. I'm not sure if I ever slept so peacefully. She made me the happiest man in the world.

But there was a problem. Jenni was also Catholic and in the Catholic tradition, you need to get married in a church for it to be recognized by the Church. Otherwise, you need to have it blessed by a priest. Months before our wedding day, we asked our priest about having our marriage blessed and were told that he would bless our marriage after our civil ceremony—a standard arrangement. We even set a date with the priest for the marriage blessing and asked our parents and grandparents to be there.

But immediately after our wedding, as Jenni worked full-time and still found time to help me with the campaign, we got a phone call that dramatically changed our plans. It was our priest and he asked us to come into his office. Jenni sensed something was wrong, but I told her not to worry. Jenni collected our marriage license and baptismal paperwork to bring to the meeting. When we got to his office, we heard stunning news: He would not bless our marriage after all. "If you worked in a factory and Jenni was a waitress down the street," he explained, "I'd bless your marriage. But because you're running for office, and with your stance on a woman's choice, I can't do it." Jenni became nauseous and rushed out of the room, tears streaming down her face. After she left, I turned to the priest. "Why?" He was getting complaints from other parishioners, he said. Despite our desire to have our marriage recognized by the Church, despite my years as an active, if imperfect, Catholic, our priest refused to bless our marriage until "six months from now." In the end, our marriage wasn't blessed for over a year. I looked back in my Iraq journal during this time. It gave me strength to reread the notes I had taken on Chaplain Murphy's Sermon on Christmas back in 2003. He told the story of St. Joan of Arc and how she was abandoned by those who should have stood by her. She said, "It's better to be alone with God. His friendship will not fail me or His counsel or His love. In His strength, I will dare and dare and dare until I die."

After the election, I finally talked about all this over lunch with my good friend Bishop McFadden, the auxiliary bishop at the Archdiocese of Philadelphia. I told him what happened, and he was visibly upset. He asked why I hadn't called him at the time. "I didn't want to ask any favors." He was compassionate and sincere, and his humanity reminded me why I love our Church. Although Jenni and I struggled with our faith as a result of this ordeal, we have forgiven our priest and the Church, and have moved on. Today, we are raising our daughter in the Catholic faith. But it wasn't the last time my views on a woman's right to choose were held against me.

Months later as Jenni and I exited Sunday Mass one evening, Mike Fitzpatrick's father, Jim (who wasn't a member of our parish), and a throng of supporters harassed us as we walked down the church steps, where they were handing out misleading campaign literature about my pro-choice views. Jenni was eight months pregnant and I pulled her close. By sending hecklers to my church, Fitzpatrick had crossed over the line of acceptable tactics. He made it personal.

Fitzpatrick was trying to suggest that I could not be a good Catholic while also being pro-choice. But I don't think it's my place to legislate my religious beliefs. Besides, the Democratic Party, at its best, embodies the core tenets of my faith. Living up to the ideals of my party means helping create a society that's more decent, equal, and just—a society that more closely observes Christ's teachings on treating others with dignity and respect. It's those teachings that are at the heart of what I believe in as a Catholic, a Democrat, and an American. And it is those teachings that I tried to place at the center of my campaign.

•

As the general election campaign heated up, one strategic lesson came from Jenni's grandfather Henry Martin, a staunch Republican. He had been a naval officer in 1942, at a time when America, outgunned in the Pacific and bloodied from the Japanese attacks on Pearl Harbor, needed a win. Mr. Martin was on the ship where the Americans rigged their small planes to take extra fuel, so they could take the offensive in what would come to be known as the Dolittle raid, after Colonel Jimmy Doolittle. It was the first U.S. air raid on the Japanese mainland during World War II. Strategically, the damage would be minimal, but emotionally, it would bolster America's fighting spirit. Like with the Doolittle Raid, I felt strongly that we needed to let the Democrats—severely outnumbered in our district by tens of thousands of voters—know that we were going to win. Our first two debates, as early as August 2006, cleared that right up.

But even before our debates began, a controversy was sparked. A few minutes into a national telephone conference call on Iraq with Senator John Kerry and newspaper reporters, we got a hostile question from Fitzpatrick's congressional chief of staff—which was surprising especially because there are strict laws regulating the role government employees can play in political campaigns. "When is Pat Murphy going to debate Congressman Fitzpatrick? Why won't he answer the congressman's challenge to debate?" he ranted. Just that week, Fitzpatrick had received our hand-delivered letter agreeing to the debates and the dates they proposed. This was a stunt and Senator Kerry knew it, responding on the line, "I've never seen an opposing party in a campaign hijack their opponents' teleconference before. This is a first." Senator Kerry and I answered a few more questions, signed off, and then reporters quickly turned and asked Fitzpatrick's chief of staff if he was on a government phone, getting paid on government time, and acting on behalf of the congressman. He denied it all. When asked later to comment on his chief of staff's tactic, Fitzpatrick said, "I'm proud of him."

Our debates gave voters plenty of time to size us up side by side, a benefit for me considering I had little name recognition. But the debates also gave Fitzpatrick the opportunity to get me on the record on hot-button issues for use in campaign mailings and television commercials. Since I had no political record as a state representative or member of a school board, he needed to draw me out, a job that was made easier because the debates were held mostly on his turf—in traditionally Republican-friendly settings like the chamber of commerce.

The first debate was held literally down the street from where Fitzpatrick grew up, at a small conservative radio station, partly owned by Merrill Reese, the voice of the Philadelphia Eagles. Even though the debate took place in a studio with just a handful of people present, we still got volunteers to show up holding "Murphy for Congress" signs outside the building as we drove in, just to set the tone. Although the debate reached just 10,000 of the 600,000 voters in the district, I knew that if I made one misstatement, Fitzpatrick would replay it on the air again and again, "killing me in the cradle"—using his financial advantage to bury me.

As I stood in the studio, I joked with Merrill Reese about my time as an Eagles security guard and reading his book, *"It's Gooooood!"* years earlier. I felt the pressure, but I wasn't going to let them see me sweat. Several seconds before we went on the air, the radio host, obviously trying to rattle me, told me he was supporting Fitzpatrick. His comment didn't help my nerves, but I just smiled and said, "That's nice." Before we even went on the air, the phone lines were full.

The most heated moment came when a caller asked, "Would you support an Israeli preemptive strike against Iran?" After Mike gave his answer, I followed up in an effort to draw him out on his foreign policy views on preemption.

> ME: . . . you're saying that [Israel] should be able to go into Iran, right now, today, against Iran?

> Fitzpatrick: If Israel believes it's in their self-interest.
>
> Me: . . . This is exactly my problem with career politicians. . . . We have politicians who want to talk very tough during an election year. . . . Israel is absolutely our greatest Democratic ally in the Middle East, we need to maintain that . . . special relationship with Israel. [But] we should be funding diplomatic efforts . . . instead of trying to spread more war in that region.

It was important to me to draw a distinction between my support for strong and principled diplomacy and what I saw as Mike's dangerous saber-rattling.

When Mike asked if I'd debate him again the following week, I said I was happy to; but this time, it had to take place in neutral territory. That first debate was probably a draw, although I benefited from being the underdog, an unknown debating a United States congressman. We felt each other out, like two boxers in the first round grappling and getting their footwork down. The second debate was where I connected my first punch and set the tone for the rest of the campaign. It took place on a weekday afternoon at a mainstay in our community, King's Caterers, a hall that hosted sports banquets, wedding receptions, fund-raisers, and prom dances. Outside, about twenty volunteers held Murphy signs, and one person showed up wearing a George W. Bush mask and a Fitzpatrick T-shirt that read "I Like Mike," the official Fitzpatrick campaign slogan.

As the crowd inside swelled to about three hundred, with workers hurriedly grabbing more and more seats, Fitzpatrick and

I sat on the two-foot-high stage in large chairs with high backs, a small table with a water pitcher and two glasses separating us. The moderator was Guy Petroziello, the editor of our local paper, the *Bucks County Courier Times.* Guy is a conservative, but he's a journalist first and a Republican second. I knew that, unlike the previous moderator, Guy would be fair.

He stood at the podium and started us off. Fitzpatrick opened. Sitting down, he gave a brief statement saying that he was the former county commissioner, was married with six kids, and was working hard in Congress. When it was my turn to speak, I stood up with the microphone in hand, faced the audience, and let them know why I was in this race.

As I was answering Guy's first question, Fitzpatrick's campaign manager, Mike Oscar, sitting in the front row with the rest of his staff, interrupted me. Rising from his chair, he said I had violated an official debate rule by paraphrasing Fitzpatrick's stance on an issue. My response was direct, confrontational, and swift. I looked down from the stage and said, "If you want to come up here and hold your candidate's hand, I'll debate both of you." The audience members, at least the hundred or so who were supporting me, loved it and rose to their feet. Guy quickly tried to calm things down.

After it was all over, I was approached by a number of people who said they felt confident I'd win the race. They couldn't believe someone was finally standing up to the Republican machine in Bucks County. It was a defining moment and it set the right tone—our team wasn't backing down from anyone.

Jenni was upset with me for going after Fitzpatrick's campaign manager. Mr. Oscar wasn't a bad guy. But I assured Jenni that I needed to send a message, that he happened to be its recipient, and that I hoped he wouldn't take it personally.

I had less respect for other Fitzpatrick aides.

At a later debate outside the *Doylestown Intelligencer* newspaper headquarters, one of his top campaign workers, his field director, literally punched one of our volunteers in the back—a sequence of events caught on videotape and later shown in the dramatic documentary *Taking the Hill*, by Brent and Craig Renault, a duo that followed four nonincumbent veteran candidates running for Congress from across the United States. Such behavior was typical for some of Fitzpatrick's supporters. They thought they could just push us around. When our lawn signs were ripped down, we'd go right back and put another up in its place the next day, even though we knew we didn't have enough money to win a war of lawn sign attrition.

A lighter moment came during a debate on Michael Smerconish's radio show. Smerconish, a Republican from Bucks County whose show and books I enjoyed, was always fair. During our debate on his show, he instructed Fitzpatrick and me that we were going into what he called the "Lightning Round." During this round, he asked simple questions requiring yes or no answers, or thumbs-up or thumbs-down. He asked Fitzpatrick, "The movie *Caddyshack*, thumbs-up or -down?" An enthusiastic two thumbs-up to most Americans, but to Fitzpatrick, it was "thumbs-down." Stunned, Republican host Smerconish tried to rehabilitate him, inquiring, "How about back in college, thumbs-up then?" Fidgeting, Fitzpatrick mumbled yes, back then he'd give it a thumbs-up. When I was asked about *Animal House*, I quickly gave a smiling "two thumbs-up and two thumbs-up for *Caddyshack*, at least I have that going for me," directly referencing a line from *Caddyshack*, one of Jenni's favorite movies.

But light moments like these were rare. As I was quickly learning, politics is a blend of two extremes: idealism of the highest order and bare-knuckle clashes of the lowest. That lesson would be reinforced in the final weeks of the campaign.

All In

My campaign manager, Scott Fairchild, had a thing about the Kenny Rogers song "The Gambler." He sang it under his breath all day long: "You got to know when to hold 'em, know when to fold 'em . . ." So I wasn't surprised when he came to me in late August with a bold proposal. Because Fitzpatrick had enough money to "kill me in the cradle" and might decide to do so anytime now, Scott suggested the extremely risky option that we go on the offensive and buy television ads immediately. We didn't have enough money to keep the ads up for long, but it would allow me to introduce myself to the voters, and define what I stood for, before Fitzpatrick or his friends at the Republican National Committee did it for me by overpowering us with television ads.

His "riverboat gambling" strategy proved to be brilliant, especially when coupled with our aggressive scheduling—attending as many fairs, parades, community days, and flea markets as possible.

As my name recognition and favorable ratings from voters shot up, more people became engaged in the campaign. Further, when Fitzpatrick and the Republican National Committee's attacks started in late fall, they didn't stick as well because voters already knew me.

In the meantime, as the leaves fell and the weather grew colder, we scraped by, saving every dollar we could. Scott was like a bulldog when it came to cost savings. He literally wouldn't even buy heating oil for our campaign office, instead instructing everyone to wear sweaters and bring in cheap, portable heaters. His mantra was, "Every $500 buys us a commercial on network television and every $100 a cable TV ad. A dozen voters may see that commercial and be swayed by it. If you don't want to lose those dozen votes, don't waste $100."

I was soon off on what we called the "Bucks Blitz"—a three-day public tour of fifty-four municipalities. My partner was Phil Lorenzon, a twenty-six-year-old Virginia Tech grad from Doylestown and a sports fanatic like me. We must have drunk fifty coffees and eaten twenty BLTs and twenty pieces of pie at diners and homes. It was probably my favorite three straight days of the campaign—not just because I had a chance to talk to lots of voters, but because it was the first time in months I didn't have to do call time.

•

One day we received notice that Fitzpatrick was holding a press conference outside the Abrams Hebrew School in Yardley, where he was going to call on me to "stand strong with Israel." Throughout the campaign, I'd pledged my support for Israel, so this was a political trick. I also knew we had just lost a hero from Bucks County, Michael Levin, who had been killed weeks earlier in Lebanon as a paratrooper in the Israeli Defense Forces.

He was home in Pennsylvania on leave when Israel was attacked and he rushed back to defend his adopted homeland and stand with his team.

Having heard the anti-Semitic rhetoric in Baghdad mosques and visited the German concentration camp at Dachau, I wasn't going to stand for a lecture on the importance of supporting Israel in their fight against terrorism. If he was going to call me out, I was going to make him do it to my face. So I showed up at his press conference and challenged his assertions directly.

But verbal assaults were not the only kind our campaign came to know. Incredibly, during one of the last debates outside the Palisades High School, Mike Fitzpatrick's father, Jim, allegedly pulled a Swiss Army knife on one of our campaign volunteers. The volunteer, a gentle middle-aged family man who was one of the nicest people I'd ever met, had been peaceably standing with his hands on one of our campaign signs and was terrified. Mr. Fitzpatrick had opened his knife, held it toward our volunteer, and said, "You know what this is. How about if I cut this sign into little pieces?"

Inside the school for the debate, I had no idea what happened until later that night. The next morning, I called our volunteer, who was still shaken up about the incident. He recounted the story and said, "Patrick, I'm not like you, I don't know how to respond in situations like that. My palms were sweating." My heart sank at how ugly this campaign was getting.

Outraged, I asked the volunteer if he had called the police and found he already had the night before. The state police came and a trooper went into the high school audience during the debate. I didn't notice because I was on stage, with the lights glaring, and couldn't see the audience too well. The state police trooper confiscated Mr. Fitzpatrick's knife, but he was never arrested. Even so, I was proud of our volunteer for doing the right thing by calling the police.

•

Mike also found people who were willing to lie about my service record. One of his supporters wrote a letter to the editor, printed in the *Bucks County Courier Times,* claiming I was only in the air-conditioned headquarters in the Green Zone in Iraq while others were doing the real fighting. Another veteran, Kevin Kelly, an air force major and chairman of the Philadelphia Young Republicans, stood outside the Newtown VFW hall during a Fitzpatrick press conference and claimed I was mischaracterizing my service record and was not a combat veteran:

> I've heard Patrick speak a few times, saying that he wasn't sure what his mission was over there . . . he is fundamentally mischaracterizing what his mission was over there. Giving the perception that he was out there, in the streets, every day with the troops, I don't think that's what his mission was. I understand I think that he was a lawyer. . . . To mischaracterize it that he was out on the ground, speaking with the Iraqis every day, dodging bullets on the street, I don't believe that's a true assessment. It does a disservice to the people over there doing that . . . Patrick Murphy . . . was not a frontline fighter. . . . It's honorable, but it seems to me that you have frontline guys and rear guard guys. . . . You've got frontline guys here. It just seems to me that Patrick Murphy wasn't one of them.

I never said I was a hero. I'm not. In fact, I took great pains to let people know that. I just did the job I was asked to do by my country—nothing more, nothing less. But I was not about to let anyone Swift Boat me. I did not disapprove of veterans standing up for their beliefs. Veterans have as much a right to fight for a policy they believe in as anyone else. But I disapprove of veterans attacking other veterans' service with personal attacks and smears. We don't get paid much in the military, but we're a proud bunch and believe in the honor of our service—and our honor should never be cheapened through such stunts.

The Fitzpatrick camp was not prepared for us to fight back quickly and fiercely. First, John Kerry himself defended me, issuing a statement: "I have news for Mike Fitzpatrick. In war, bullets don't differentiate between lawyers and medics, enlisted men and officers." Then Wesley Clark came to my defense publicly on a conference call. We also held a rally and press conference to repudiate the Fitzpatrick campaign's lies with dozens of veterans of all ages. My old battle buddy from Iraq, Captain Koby Langley, selflessly drove up from his home in Virginia to stand with me.

But as angry as I was with the veterans who were trying to Swift Boat me, this was between Fitzpatrick and me. How could this tactic be condoned by a guy who had never worn a military uniform? Fitzpatrick tried to deny he had done anything wrong, since the smears didn't come from his mouth. When a reporter caught up with him afterward, he said, "In no way, shape, or form would I ever question Pat Murphy's service to our country. I recognize and appreciate Pat's service to our country as much as anyone." Sure, he just held a press conference and put veterans behind his podium to smear my character. I didn't appreciate that kind of "recognition."

Taking my defense to the airwaves, I looked into the camera, with my photographs from Iraq flashing in the background, stating firmly, "Once you've seen things like this, my opponent's lies and smears don't matter too much. What matters to me is changing the course in Iraq, and bringing our men and women home." I stood behind my ads; in every one I said what I felt in my heart. Fitzpatrick hid behind some deep-voiced announcer until the end of his television commercials when he legally had to appear and approve his negative messages.

One of his negative ads claimed I had never been a prosecutor. While active-duty personnel cannot get involved in politics, I urgently asked now general Patrick Finnegan, my former boss at West Point, simply to confirm that I had been a prosecutor at both West Point and Fort Bragg. We didn't have time to wait for an official opinion from the Pentagon. As Mark Twain once said, "A lie can travel halfway round the world while the truth is putting on its shoes." So I was grateful that General Finnegan didn't take the easy way out and hide behind some army regulation. He was still the leader I knew him to be and he corroborated my service as a prosecutor. But Fitzpatrick didn't stop the ads. The father of the sexually assaulted six-year-old girl I had defended wrote a letter on my behalf, reliving his family's pain just to help clear my name. *This is the state of American politics?*

I attacked Mike Fitzpatrick, too, of course. I attacked his votes in Congress, I attacked his position on the Iraq War, on Washington fiscal policy, and on embryonic stem cell research. He and his Bush-Republican allies attacked my service in the military and my credentials as a prosecutor, and took just about any other cheap shot they could dig up from my personal life. That was the difference.

When I saw Fitzpatrick at a candidates' forum in Buckingham in the final days of the campaign on October 25, I confronted him publicly about his false ad. "You, sir, are a liar and a coward for hiding behind these ads." I didn't like using those kinds of words, but I was not going to let him get away with it.

•

In the last few weeks of the campaign we were fortunate to have high-profile Democrats campaign for us. Earlier Congresswoman Tammy Baldwin, the first openly gay woman in Congress, had spoken for me when most politicos wouldn't give me a chance. Now, Senator John Kerry spoke at my alma matter, Bucks County Community College. Senator Barack Obama came and was inspiring. And Governor Ed Rendell, who faced his own re-election, also helped.

But the most memorable visit was on the afternoon of Wednesday, October 11, as four thousand people gathered on Mill Street, just down the street from my house, to hear the forty-second president of the United States. "Do we have a great candidate or what?" President Clinton asked as he took the podium. "When you look at this young man and you realize the life he's lived and the service he rendered and the fact that his opponent actually had the gall to try to pull a Swift Boat on him." At that, the crowd started booing. Fitzpatrick's attacks on me, he said, were like those of a "mangy dog." And "the problem with mangy dogs," he said, "is you can run 'em out of the kennel one time and they might scare people off, but after a while you just see it for what it is: just a mangy old dog. That's what this is." The crowd roared, waving "Murphy for Congress" signs.

A conservative newspaper columnist at the *Bucks County CourierTimes,* J. D. Mullane, had written weeks earlier that if the national Democrats were serious about my race, they needed to bring the big gun he called "Bubba." Not only did President Bill Clinton come, but it was the most electric and inspirational rally I have ever seen. Just like he did at King's College ten years earlier, he worked the crowd afterward, shaking hands, signing autographs, posing for pictures, being his gregarious self. When President Clinton was finally escorted away, he huddled in a nearby coffee shop to grab a cup of coffee to go. I asked for one last favor. In the coffee shop he made a special phone call to Shelbie Oppenheimer from my cell phone. She was a huge admirer of President Clinton. Her husband, Jeff, said when she heard the message President Clinton left on their answering machine, she lit up. Of all the hundreds of hours of call time during the campaign, that call was by far the most meaningful.

•

By late October, polls showed that Fitzpatrick and I were neck and neck—even though we were being outspent by close to $3 million. Fitzpatrick's campaign raised $3.1 million, most of it from political action committees (PACs). The National Republican Congressional Committee also spent $3.6 million to defend his seat—mostly by attacking me. Our campaign raised $2.3 million, the majority of it from more than twenty-one thousand individual donors—like my former neighbor Frances Nell—and from many of the more than four hundred thousand visitors to our Web site. Rahm Emanuel and the Democratic Congressional Campaign Committee spent $1.5 million. It was one of the most expensive races in the country, and the most expensive in Bucks County history. *Would I fall in the 2 percent who beat their opponent while being outspent?*

With a week to go, Scott Fairchild and Carrie James walked into my office and shut the door. They had a simple question: "Are you willing to go into campaign debt to win, even if it means settling up afterward out of your own pocket?" We were days away and so close. Financially, I couldn't afford to take the campaign into debt. I had already taken a partial leave of absence from the law firm and my savings were nil. Jenni and I also had a mortgage and a new baby on the way within weeks. But I remembered being disheartened learning of candidates who had money left over in close but unsuccessful races. I wanted to leave it all out on the ice. I approved $140,000 of campaign debt, an obligation I knew I'd have to pay back. I was now "all in."

•

The final days of the race were rough. The Republicans flooded the state with operatives as part of their vaunted "72-hour program" to seal the deal on close elections. When I found out that John McCain was coming to campaign for Fitzpatrick on the Saturday before the election, I asked Colonel Jack Murtha if he could come on the same day to speak at my VFW hall in Bristol Township, and he did. The next day both Murtha and McCain made the front pages of local papers.

There were still doubters. On local television two nights before Election Day, a high-level Democratic pundit, Mark Alderman, was asked which Democrats would win the three Philadelphia suburban races. He replied, "Patrick Murphy will be the only one who doesn't win." I watched his comments during a rebroadcast at around 1:00 a.m., as Jenni lay in bed sound asleep next to me. I stewed, remembering what Teddy Roosevelt said about the credit belonging not to the critic but to the man in the arena. *I'm going to show him.* (Today we're friends.)

The morning before Election Day, I went to the Warminster train station to campaign. It was my sixth time at that station. Fitzpatrick was there that day, too. It was the first time I had seen him there. Days earlier, he had gone to the Levittown Train

Station and confronted Sara Schaumburg, our tiny 5'1" field organizer, with the remark, "No use in you being out here. Your guy is going down." Sara, who fit right in with our respectful but combative team, didn't miss a beat. "Not according to this, Congressman," she said, handing him a photocopy of the recent endorsement of my candidacy in the *Bucks County Courier Times.*

On the Warminster train platform that day, Fitzpatrick and I handed out literature to the same commuters, a couple of feet apart. We were both worn down, thinner than when the campaign started, and fatigued like two boxers in the last round of an eighteen-month fight. Those commuters didn't see the bottom of my black dress shoes, but there was a huge hole on each sole, a testament to the months of hard work we had put in. Those torn shoes were a badge of honor. They now sit in my congressional office in Washington as a reminder of what we accomplished.

Late that night, Seth Frotman and I met up with Chris Norbeck at the Great American Diner in Bensalem, the township on the northern border of Philadelphia. We all I ordered and I went to shake hands and meet the other diners. When I finished twenty minutes later and came back to the table, Seth and Chris were almost done eating. Because I had skipped lunch, I devoured the BBQ ribs that were sitting cold on my plate. Afterward, Chris went out to place lawn signs all over Northeast Philadelphia with our high school buddies. I sat in the car with Seth and told him how proud I was of our team. I felt like I did the night before I left Baghdad. I was exhausted, both mentally and physically, and just incredibly proud of what our team had accomplished. I told Seth I was so proud of everyone, it didn't matter if we won or not. Frankly, I must have been delirious to say I didn't care about winning.

We then drove to our last stop, the International Brotherhood of Electrical Workers local 269. Filling their standing-room-only union hall were more than three hundred members, mostly clad in jeans and sweatshirts. I took the podium, hugging Steve Aldrich, a 6'3" mountain of a man who backed me early on when many others did not. It was my last speech and I gave it from my heart, with a voice so hoarse I had to yell to be heard. Looking into their eyes, I told them we were on the cusp of greatness—that if we stood together tomorrow, against all the odds, we'd be standing victorious, standing against a Bush administration that was hostile to working families, and standing up for a new direction in this country.

On Election Day, November 7, 2006, we ran a field program that set an incredible record for a congressional race. Under Scott's leadership and an incredible display of teamwork, 1,200 volunteers went out that day and knocked on over 140,000 doors. Scott's field program was peaking at just the right time. After voting together first thing in the morning, Jenni, who was eight months pregnant, went to the Republican-leaning polling places in central and northern Bucks County while I raced around lower and central Bucks County visiting voters at other polling places. Because I'm a little superstitious, I had lunch with Dick Doran again, as I had in the primary, and again I couldn't bring myself to eat too much.

After lunch, I went back to the office to thank the volunteers, my voice still hoarse, just as a batch was leaving to get out the vote. I returned to thank volunteers throughout the day, and if I couldn't make it back, my father spoke to them on my behalf. It seemed as if friends from every stage of my life had come out of the woodwork to help. Watching friends I hadn't seen in years door-knocking was humbling, and gave us hope that something special was happening. Few encapsulated our all-hands-on-deck approach better than Kevin Kruse, a highly successful, buttoned-down businessman and father of three from Bucks County who was transformed on Election Day into a frenetic, hard-charging volunteer, grabbing lists of addresses and furiously running door-to-door, his business attire soaked in sweat. Meanwhile, my sixty-year-old mother stood outside the entrance of St. Ann's Church in Bristol all day and asked all the voters as they went inside, "Can you please vote for my son Patrick?" We won that polling place.

By 8:00 p.m., when the polls closed, I was absolutely spent. That was my finish line, and Jenni and I snuck away to our room at the Langhorne Sheraton Hotel, giving few besides Scott and my brother our room number. Jenni and I lay on the bed. We had given it every ounce of energy we had. But we were too anxious to nap, and too nervous to watch the results, so I flipped through the TV channels. I felt like a winner, but I knew it'd be close, and I knew I was still the underdog.

As the tallies came in, it went back and forth like a roller coaster. Depending on what numbers were being called in, we were either jubilant or somber. We were barely winning some Democratic strongholds, but almost winning some Republican strongholds. By 11:00 p.m., it was still too close to call. Then, with almost a quarter million votes cast, we edged ahead by about one thousand votes with nearly all precincts reporting. I was too exhausted to say or do much, except to thank Scott and the team and hug Jenni.

Fitzpatrick called our Democratic chairman in Bucks County, John Cordisco, and said he was going home to bed and wasn't going to concede. I wasn't sure exactly what to do. Then my phone rang. It was President Clinton asking about our results. I was honored he had taken the time to call, and since I had him on the line, I gave him the numbers and asked his advice. The former president was clear: "Don't let those bastards take away your victory. You go down to that hall and declare yourself the winner. Let the press sort it out."

That is exactly what I did. Jenni and I walked down to the Sheraton ballroom around 1:30 a.m. Hundreds of supporters were packed inside. By the time we entered, news had spread that we were up. We walked through the crowd, giving high fives and bear hugs, and finally made it to the stage, where Jenni and I were greeted by the rest of our family amid chants of "Murphy! Murphy!"

I took the podium and looked out on the people who had been with me all the way—folks like Tim Persico, Alan Sheriff, Chris Norbeck, and Seth Frotman. My eyes teared up as I began to speak.

> When I said that I wanted to run for Congress, few gave me a chance. They said: Patrick, there's no way the son of a Philadelphia cop and legal secretary—who grew up in a row home in the Northeast—could win a seat in Congress.
>
> But you believed that we needed a change. You believed we could do better. And—against incredible odds—you believed in me. . . .
>
> For me the journey began in 138-degree heat, on the streets of Baghdad. We were sent to battle without enough troops and without a plan to win the peace. Nineteen guys from my unit, who never made it home, deserved a government as honest and as decent as they were. And when I got back from Iraq, I saw that we needed change here at home, too. . . .
>
> So I stand before you today as your congressman-elect more humbled, more hopeful, and more assured in my faith in the American people than I ever could have imagined 534 days ago.

> Thank you for your support. Thank you for your trust. And I promise you one thing—I will make you proud.

In the end, we won one of the country's closest races by 0.6 points, or 1,518 votes, in what was rightfully described as the biggest political upset in the history of the Eighth Congressional District. Even though we lost Bucks County by over 1,000 votes, Northeast Philadelphia came through with 950 and the small section of Montgomery County that lies in our district provided 1,500 more. We now affectionately call that sliver of Montgomery County the "Murphy Margin."

•

The next day, I pulled myself out of bed at 5 a.m. after about two hours of sleep and went dutifully back to where so many mornings had started, predawn at the Bensalem train station of Cornwells Heights. It was pouring rain, and my worn-down shoes were waterlogged. "I didn't think you were going to win, but I voted for you anyway," one passenger, Georgee Thevervelil of Bensalem, told me. "Thanks for proving me wrong." Standing on the platform after the 8:53 a.m. train pulled out of the station, I looked around. There were no more hands to shake. The campaign was over. We had taken the Hill. It was just the beginning.

Epilogue

The future does not belong to those who are content with today, apathetic toward common problems and their fellow man alike, timid and fearful in the face of bold projects and new ideas. Rather, it will belong to those who can blend passion, reason and courage in a personal commitment to the great enterprises and ideals of American society.

—Robert F. Kennedy

On Monday, March 26, 2007, two months after I was sworn into Congress, I took the floor of the House of Representatives. I walked to the well beneath the Speaker's chair, and I looked out on the crowded chamber. Hundreds of spectators and congressional colleagues lined the elegant gallery, with its plush blue carpet and rows of brown leather chairs. It was a different perspective than I was used to. No longer was I the dutiful soldier, executing the orders of my commanders. No longer was I just a political warrior, throwing and taking verbal jabs on the campaign trail. Now I had another responsibility—to help put our nation on the right course.

The Iraq War funding bill I rose to address that day imposed a twelve-month timeline for withdrawal from Iraq. Not all Democrats agreed with the bill. Some argued that with our troops in harm's way we shouldn't place any restrictions on the president. Others felt that the bill didn't go far enough in ending the war. For me, the choice was clear. This was what I had run for Congress to do—help bring about a change of course in Iraq—and I did not plan to miss the opportunity.

Looking out on the chamber, I made one of the final arguments before the vote.

> We had a saying in the army: "Lead. Follow. Or get out of the way." Well, in the past four years, the Republican-led Congress followed. They had their chance and they followed lockstep as this president led our country into an open-ended commitment refereeing a religious civil war. For the last four years, this Republican Congress followed lockstep as my fellow soldiers continued to die in Iraq, without a clear mission, without benchmarks to determine success, without a clear timeline for coming home.
>
> In the last four years, the Republican Congress followed this president, as thousands of brave American soldiers returned home in coffins, draped with our American flag. . . .

> Mr. Speaker, with this bill, with this vote, we mark the end of that era.
>
> To those on the other side of the aisle who are opposed, I want to ask you the same questions that my gunner asked me when I was leading a convoy up and down Ambush Alley one day. He said, "Sir, what are we doing over here? What's our mission? When are these Iraqis going to come off the sidelines and fight for their own country?"
>
> So to my colleagues across the aisle—your taunts about supporting our troops ring hollow if you are still unable to answer those questions now, four years later.

Giving our country a foreign policy that is just as smart and savvy as the troops on the ground overseas is our duty in Washington. But the political pundits predicted that, with only a slim majority in Congress, the Democrats didn't have enough votes in the House of Representatives to pass a bill that included a binding timeline. In the end, after the votes were counted, enough of us came together and the bill squeezed by with a razor-thin four-vote margin, out of more than four hundred cast. Soon afterward it went to the Senate, where most of us expected it to die. Remarkably, it again passed. This was a significant moment, the first time during this conflict that a war-funding bill had significant conditions attached to it. At last, Congress was standing up to the president, reasserting the rights and responsibilities with which it is charged by the Constitution. As NAACP chairman Julian Bond said, "If you have an administration that's reckless, you can't have an opposition that's spineless." For the first time in more than six years, Congress was beginning to show some spine.

But tragically, on May 1, 2007, four years after his speech on the flight deck of the USS *Abraham Lincoln* beneath a "Mission

Accomplished" banner, President Bush used the second veto of his presidency to kill our binding legislation, his first having been used to stop stem cell research. Our nation—and the world—was being held hostage to the pride of a single man who refused to acknowledge and correct his catastrophic mistake.

Three weeks later, the House of Representatives again debated an Iraq War funding bill. This time there were no timelines to bring our troops home. It was the day before the Memorial Day weekend and political strategists cautioned me that a vote against it would be used in an opponent's campaign commercial sixteen months later to claim I was "not funding the troops." But I could not in good conscience give President Bush another blank check in this war. The night before this vote I was torn. I spoke and prayed with Father Tom O'Hara, a friend and current president of King's College who happened to be visiting Washington. He gently advised, "Vote your conscience." I also spoke by phone to my Iraq buddy RV, who was now finishing his second year as a West Point cadet, who believed I should stick to my guns, and my brother, J.J., who reminded me of our dad's saying, "If you don't stand for something, you'll fall for anything." Lastly, following our daily routine when I'm away from home, I called Jenni late that night. She was in bed at our home and I was in Washington, but I couldn't sleep. Jenni let me know she believed in my judgment to do what was right.

The next day I saw one of my best friends in Congress, former New York prosecutor and fellow freshman Democrat Mike Acuri. He said, "Where you at, Murph?" I looked him in the eye and told him I was voting against the funding and gave him my rationale. Then Congressman Acuri, a former college football player, said something I'll never forget. "I'm not voting for it either. If you play sports afraid to get hurt, you will get hurt. If you vote by calculating whether you may get voted out of office, you will get voted out of office. I'm glad to hear you're voting your conscience, too." We both voted against the bill, along with 142 others. It passed anyway.

•

In 2003, when RV first asked me what our mission was in Iraq, roughly four hundred Americans had been killed in Iraq. Now, the death toll is ten times higher. For generations to come, historians will scour White House documents—whenever this secrecy-obsessed White House releases them—to understand exactly what happened, exactly how our nation was led into the worst foreign policy blunder in American history. It will be their task to understand how this senseless war came about. It is now our task to end it. Bringing my BOLT team home was my mission as Captain Murphy; bringing all our troops home is my mission as Congressman Murphy.

Our continued occupation in Iraq advances neither U.S. nor Iraqi nor the region's interests. In fact, it is a grave liability. Our presence enables the Iraqis to rely too heavily on us, delaying the day when they finally get off the sidelines and bring a measure of order and stability to their country. It diminishes our moral standing, which is the foundation of our global leadership. And it fans the flames of extremism, making it far harder to eliminate the terrorist threat.

As I write this, the heirs of 9/11 terrorist Mohammed Atta are no doubt plotting their next attack in the hills of Pakistan and Afghanistan, where al Qaeda has regrouped, and is now stronger than at any time since that Tuesday morning in 2001. It is time to pull out of Iraq so we can wage the war we should have waged after September 11, the war against our sworn enemy, al Qaeda. During World War II, President Franklin D. Roosevelt pursued a strategy of "Germany First." America must pursue a strategy of "al Qaeda first."

•

We have to end this war in Iraq so we can finally get back to addressing the domestic challenges we face here at home. This war could cost the American people nearly $2 trillion through the next decade. The war has already cost folks in my own district $1.3 billion in tax revenues. Just imagine the different ways we could be investing that astronomical amount of money. With that money, we could have paid for health care for more than three hundred thousand people or built more than ninety elementary schools or hired more than twenty thousand elementary school teachers. If truth was the first casualty of this war, our domestic priorities were the second.

Working-class Americans are first among those who have lost out during the Bush years. Politicians often invoke the middle class to burnish their everyman credentials. For me, fighting for the middle class isn't about politics—it's personal. I will never forget where I came from. My dad was a cop for twenty-two years, my mom was a legal secretary, and my best buddy Chris Norbeck is a Teamster who works for Budweiser (and don't even think about ordering a Miller when you're out with him). Fighting for middle-class Americans means fighting for the people I grew up with in Northeast Philly and now have the honor of representing.

Some argue that even talking about helping middle-class Americans raises the specter of class warfare. But as one of the wealthiest Americans, Warren Buffett, has said, "[There] is class warfare. And my class is winning, but they shouldn't be." In

Congress, I've made it my mission to do something about this, to make our policies more equitable. In my first year in Washington, I've fought to make health care more affordable by making it legal for the federal government to negotiate with drug companies so we can drive down the cost of prescription drugs. I've fought to cover 11 million children and fully reimburse doctors serving Medicare patients. I've fought to raise the minimum wage for the first time in a decade, and strengthen our unions by fighting for Americans' rights to organize and collectively bargain with their employers. My dad has been a member of the Fraternal Order of Police and AFSCME, and I know how much being a union man did for our whole family.

But middle-class Americans will continue taking hits even after the Bush administration leaves office unless we start acting with a sense of urgency. Part of our national response has to be investing in the jobs of the future. Take, for example, Fairless Hills, nestled along the Delaware River in Bucks County. At its peak in the 1970s, nearly ten thousand people worked at the U.S. Steel facility there. As has happened elsewhere in this country, sharp declines in steel manufacturing forced U.S. Steel to shut down most of its Fairless operations, costing thousands of good-paying jobs. By the early 1990s, fewer than one hundred workers remained and much of the land was neglected—leaving a large part of the site an environmentally compromised "brownfield."

But today, the site is vibrant again as thousands of "green collar" manufacturing jobs are being created to make this town one of America's leading green energy hubs. Triggered by economic incentives and a public-private partnership, some of the best alternative energy companies in the world are being lured to Bucks County. It is now home to a Spanish windmill manufacturer that builds hundreds of turbines that are shipped across

North America to create wind power; a South Korean manufacturer that is investing millions of dollars to make solar energy more viable to both commercial and residential customers; and, in Lower Bucks, a German company is building the fourth-largest solar panel field in the United States. In addition to giving a much-needed boost to our local economy, these investments help make America energy independent so we can one day stop sending $25 billion a year to the Persian Gulf, filling the coffers of hostile nations. Innovative thinking like this has helped create an economic miracle, and Congress has a responsibility to empower towns across America to follow suit.

•

But we're not going to be able to meet any of our challenges here at home or around the world unless we quit fighting one another and start coming together to fight our common problems. This is something I didn't fully appreciate as a candidate. There have even been times in Congress when I've been too partisan, and I'll work to correct that. I'm not naive. I understand that it's sometimes necessary to throw elbows and draw sharp distinctions. I know politics is a contact sport. Frankly, I enjoy the combativeness and competition.

But I've also gained a deeper appreciation over these past few months of how legislative progress actually happens in this country. In the army, I gave an order and it was carried out—or else there were consequences. In Congress, things get done by building coalitions within and across party lines. It's not easy. Thankfully, I've got some experience here. I come from a politically mixed family—Jenni and my mother are still Republicans. I've learned bipartisanship the hard way: I've slept on the couch.

In Congress, I'm proud of our Democratic family and have

worked hard to build solid relationships with Republican friends. I've joined the Blue Dog Coalition, a group of forty-seven Democrats known for reaching across the aisle and standing strong for balanced budgets and fiscal responsibility. This is an area where I believe we need urgent action. We have to pay down our $9 trillion of national debt, much of which we owe to countries like China, Japan, India, and Mexico. These countries are acting like our bankers, with China financing the cost of the Iraq War. Like a bad credit card debt, each month the United States ships roughly $21 billion abroad in interest payments alone, not even touching the principal amount due. By comparison, the federal government spends only around $5 billion a month on education. Each American owes $29,000 toward our national debt, a number that keeps rising. We need leadership and discipline to pay down our debt so we don't pass it along to our children. Now is the time to mandate pay-as-you-go budgets and enforce the Blue Dogs' commonsense fiscal principles.

National security and border security are other areas where I've worked with Republicans. When Republican congressman Phil Gingrey proposed extending the life of the School of the Americas, a controversial U.S. military institution where we train foreign soldiers, I supported him. Most Democrats, including my friend Jim McGovern, opposed the extension, citing the fact that atrocious crimes were committed years ago by foreign soldiers trained at the school. I understood my fellow Democrats' concerns, and I respect them. But I've also witnessed first-hand in Iraq why it is so important that foreign soldiers have adequate professional training in values, laws of war, and military skills. When we offer them that training, we enhance our own security rather than weaken it.

Securing our borders—the first step on the road to solving our immigration crisis—is another issue that demands bipartisanship. That's why when my colleague from Pennsylvania, Republican Charlie Dent, offered a commonsense bill to toughen border security by allowing our civil air patrol to assist law enforcement efforts, I was one of his cosponsors, and I've also fought to add three thousand new border agents and to strengthen criminal penalties for those who smuggle illegal aliens into this country.

I have also proudly stood with Democrats and Republicans to fight for our veterans. These men and women have asked for nothing except to serve this country, and this administration has betrayed them. From the scandals at Walter Reed to the cuts in veterans' benefits, it is clear that the Bush administration sees "supporting our troops" as little more than a slogan. In recent years, returning soldiers have had to fight battle after battle to get the housing and health care they need. When I was growing up, I paid a visit to the trailer where Pop-Pop lived in New Jersey, and remember it being infested with flease. No one should live like that, much less someone who proudly wore the uniform of his country.

So I have helped lead an effort to increase funding for the Department of Veterans Affairs by $6.7 billion, the largest single increase in its seventy-seven-year history. And I am doing what I can to support veterans in other ways—encouraging Iraq War veteran candidates like Jon Powers up in New York or John Boccieri in Ohio to run, or having quiet conversations with soldiers who are about to return to Iraq or meeting with the families of fallen heroes. I've also taken steps to help the forgotten heroes of the Iraq War, the Iraqis who risked their lives to help us. When our translator Alyaa needed to escape the dangers of Iraq, I was proud that my former colleagues at Cozen O'Connor fought for her to earn an educational visa to come to the United States to study. She's here today and we're still working on bringing her cousin Shaimaa over. Unfortunately, there are tens of thousands of courageous Iraqis like Alyaa who haven't been as lucky.

•

The hardest part about being a congressman is being away from Jenni and our baby daughter, Maggie, so much. Most weeks I stay in Washington, where I share a tiny apartment—like many other congressmen—with a roommate, Tim Walz, a former army command sergeant major and now a congressman from Minnesota. Jenni and Maggie stay home in Bristol, so I try to set aside weekends, especially Sundays, for family time, like those Sunday dinners at Grandmom's house when I was a kid. I've become a regular at Union Station, where I pick up the Amtrak train to go home after each workweek.

As the train leaves the station, in between catching up on reading or phone calls, I sometimes think about the city I now work in, and what an honor it is to be serving the people of Pennsylvania's Eighth Congressional District. But what I've learned in my short time there is that Washington is a place of stunning contradictions: halls of power just a few blocks away from bitter urban poverty, compassion and intelligence jostling with pettiness and arrogance, idealistic advocates competing with lobbyists for big special interests.

And yet, for all its flaws, every time I walk up those Capitol steps, there's something that inspires me. It's the idea I taught my constitutional law class at West Point—that, in this country, the people have the ability to correct our government's worst imperfections, that, while America will never be perfect, we each have the power to inch it closer toward that more perfect union—and we all have an obligation to try.

I've always done my best to live up to that idea —to live up to the prayer of St. Francis that we might each be an "instrument of God's peace." I am too imperfect to ever be a true instrument of God's peace, but I will never stop trying.

My belief in service is rooted not just in faith but in friendship. That was the secret we learned in the desert. We were in Iraq to serve our country, but we survived Iraq by serving one another. On the roof that night at Scania when we took fire, on patrols down Ambush Alley when RV spotted the IED, at the Al Bayaa courthouse in Al Rashid when Stick was guarding the window—at each of these moments, and so many others, we were putting our lives on the line not simply to carry out our nation's policy or to bring a measure of stability to the lives of ordinary Iraqis, but so that our fellow soldiers might live. As fiercely self-reliant as we are taught to be in the military, as sophisticated as our advanced individual training is, each soldier is part of something larger, whether it's a BOLT, a squad, a platoon, or a brigade. Each soldier is part of a team. Even the army paratrooper dropped behind enemy lines is dependent on his fellow soldiers for intelligence support, air cover, and an array of other services to achieve his mission. In the end, it was this sense of shared responsibility—a principle we internalized at boot camp, a truth we witnessed at war—that accounted for our survival and whatever measure of success we found in Iraq. That is the lesson my service taught me. That is the commitment nineteen members of my brigade gave their lives upholding. And that is the belief we need to reclaim in America.

Now on the front lines in Washington, I remain hopeful. Not because I trust our government to always pass perfect laws—I don't. Or because I trust our leaders to always make the right decisions—I don't. But because people from Pennsylvania to Baghdad have shown me that each of us has the ability to change our world for the better—because we all have the ability to treat others with dignity and respect, to take our jobs seriously, but never ourselves too seriously, and to be courageous even in the face of fear. Each of us has that ability—and that responsibility.

Now is a defining moment in our nation's history. America faces steep challenges at home and abroad. But I'm confident we'll meet them. Because if there's one thing I've relearned throughout my life, it's that no hill is too hard to take, so long as we climb it together.

Acknowledgments

Writing this book has been an emotional journey. There are a number of hazards in writing your own story—the hazard of selective memory, the risk of portraying yourself more favorably than events warranted, or amplifying your own role in events. And while I relied not just on my own memory but on family, friends, colleagues, my Iraq war journals, and news sources to reconstruct events and conversations, I cannot claim to have escaped all of these hazards. Further, in some places, omissions of names and personal details were made to protect privacy. But, to the best of my imperfect abilities, the way I tell this story is the way I remember it.

There are so many people to thank that it is impossible to list each of them here. But I would be remiss if I didn't acknowledge those who are so close to my heart.

To my beautiful and loving wife Jenni: We have traveled these last few years together and have been blessed with a beautiful family. I hope and pray for six or seven more decades together, and that I continue to be the man you love so selflessly. Thank you for being my best friend and giving us Maggie, who easily melts away all the pressures in the world with her beautiful smile.

To my loving family: From the strong women who led by example, including my mother, Margaret; sister, Cathy; and sister-in-law, Colleen; to my dutiful father, Jack; brother-in-law Brian; and tenacious brother, J.J., each of you have taught me what giving of yourself truly is. We continue to be there for each other no matter where life's paths take each of us. Thank you for always keeping me grounded in what's important in life; I'm honored to consider all of you you as my friends as well.

To our campaign team: Scott, Tim, Gwen, Nat, Seth, Carrie, Dan, Mads, Nate, the Bens, Phil, Mike, Brandon, Josh, Dave, Eric, Emily, Theresa, Frank, Lou, Chris, Cathy, John, Helene, Jordan, Neil, Lauren, Ed, Kevin, Pete, Wayne, Vanya, John, Bert, Paul, Jan, Alison, Jon, Jordan, Susan, Doreen, Debbie, Cynara, Tony, Brent, Kathleen, Boris, Doug, Lara, Daren, Regina, Jake, Keith, Lindsay, Jane, Adrienne, Sara, Brendan, Roberta, Sandy, Bill, Steve, Glenn, Norval, George, Anne, Brad, Fred, Daniel, Maggie, Jason, Isaac, Tom, Seth, Sophie and every other volunteer. Each of you took a chance and has sacrificed so much to bring about the change we all believe is needed in our country. I am so proud of each of you and what we have done together.

To our Democratic family: From the netroots community to our party organization, we have an incredible chance to lead and make our world an even better place for our children. I am confident that if we reach out to our Republican friends we will do just that.

To my friends: Most of you are already considered to be like my family. Thank you for always being there when I have needed you most. A special thank-you to Alan and Karen Sheriff, Jeff and Shelbie Oppenheimer, Chris and Catherine Asplan, Dick and Mary Doran, Peter Tucci, Pat O'Connor, Steve Cozen, John Park, and Chris Norbeck.

To my military brethren: From my first days in Army ROTC to my last days at Fort Bragg, you have made me the person I am. Thank you for doing what so many others in our nation are unwilling to do.

To the media: Thank you for being our much-needed fourth estate. I'd especially like to thank Brian Scheid, Brian Callaway, Gaiutra Bahadur, Rajiv Chandrasekaran, and Vivienne Walt, whose writings I drew upon and found particularly helpful. I'd also like to thank Adam Bonin, Brian Haig, Juan Arevalo, Ellen Rose, Nathan Hake, Les Sdorow, Captain Tyson Voekel, John Morgenstern, Keith Kincaid, Jim Mulhall, Pete Giangreco, Jef Pollock, Robert Zimmerman, and Congressman Bill Green for their constructive and invaluable feedback throughout the editorial process.

To Henry Holt and Company: Thank you for giving me a chance to tell a story of service that I believe needs to be told. Editor David Patterson, publisher John Sterling, and everyone at Holt has helped craft a book about a very small slice of American history.

To Esther Newberg at International Creative Management: While I had to repeatedly convince you that some folks may be interested in "an Irish Catholic Philadelphia-area Congressman," you have been one of my biggest supporters since. Thank you for helping give me a chance and believing in me.

To Adam Frankel: You have been my true partner throughout this book. I am amazed at your writing abilities and even more at your heart and commitment. I cannot thank you enough for helping me write a book that my daughter will someday read and hopefully value.

To my constituents in the Eighth Congressional District of Pennsylvania: Thank you for giving me the opportunity to serve you and our country. I hope I'm making you proud.

Jenni and I are proud that 10 percent of our book proceeds will go to the Iraq and Afghanistan Veterans of America, a nonprofit and nonpartisan veterans organization.

—Patrick J. Murphy

It is impossible to thank all the people who've been there for me throughout this process, offering support and guidance—personal and professional—at each step. But I'll try. First, there's Laura Breckenridge, whose love and support were essential to my work on this book—as they are to everything I do. I've stopped asking how I got so lucky and started just being grateful for it.

I also want to thank my parents, Ellen Perecman and Stephen and Helen Frankel; my grandparents, Irene Frankel and my late grandfather—and hero—Stan Frankel, Gershon Perecman, and my late grandmother Rivka Perecman; my great aunt Jo; and uncle Newt Minow.

I also want to thank Jon Favreau for his encouragement and understanding when this book demanded increasing amounts of my time even as our speechwriting workload on the campaign ramped up. I wouldn't have been able to take this on if he hadn't been so supportive.

A number of friends and family helped out during the course of this project. Both Nell Minow and Greg Behrman, who introduced me to Congressman Murphy, took the time to read a draft and offered thoughtful and enormously helpful guidance. I also received assistance on substantive, stylistic, or other book-related topics from Martha Minow, Ben Rhodes, Sarah Holewinski, Madhuri Kommareddi, Danielle Gray, Cody Keenan, Jenny Urizar, Carlos Monje, and Ariana Berengaut.

It's also a pleasure to acknowledge some of the friends and mentors who've helped make me the person I am today: Drew Warshaw, Dana Malman, Josh Gottheimer, Jeff Shesol, Ted Sorensen, Brian DeLeeuw, Jon Barnes, and Sarah Shepard.

Finally, I want to thank Congressman Murphy for asking me to coauthor this book with him. Over the course of our collaboration, I've developed a deep sense of admiration and respect for him. And I've come to value not just his leadership but his friendship.

—Adam Frankel

Index

Index

Index

Index

Index

Index

About the Authors

CONGRESSMAN PATRICK J. MURPHY represents Pennsylvania's Eighth District. He lives in suburban Philadelphia with his wife, Jenni, and daughter, Maggie.

ADAM FRANKEL is currently a speechwriter on Senator Barack Obama's presidential campaign. A former AIDS activist in Africa, Adam assisted President Kennedy's adviser Theodore C. Sorensen on his memoirs and has served as a fellow in the office of counterterrorism at the State Department and as a deputy project director at the Council on Foreign Relations. Adam graduated from Princeton University and received a master's degree from the London School of Economics, where he was a Fulbright Scholar.